TRAVEL

IN THE FIRST CENTURY AFTER CHRIST.

T0371212

TRAVEL

IN THE FIRST CENTURY AFTER CHRIST

WITH SPECIAL REFERENCE TO ASIA MINOR

BY

CAROLINE A. J. SKEEL,

FORMER STUDENT OF GIRTON COLLEGE, CAMBRIDGE;
LECTURER IN HISTORY, WESTFIELD COLLEGE, HAMPSTEAD.

CAMBRIDGE:
AT THE UNIVERSITY PRESS.
1901

CAMBRIDGE
UNIVERSITY PRESS

University Printing House, Cambridge CB2 8BS, United Kingdom

Published in the United States of America by Cambridge University Press, New York

Cambridge University Press is part of the University of Cambridge.

It furthers the University's mission by disseminating knowledge in the pursuit of
education, learning and research at the highest international levels of excellence.

www.cambridge.org
Information on this title: www.cambridge.org/9781107635487

© Cambridge University Press 1901

First published 1901
First paperback edition 2014

A catalogue record for this publication is available from the British Library

ISBN 978-1-107-63548-7 Paperback

PREFACE.

THIS essay was originally written in competition for the Gibson Prize founded in 1889 by Mrs J. Y. Gibson in connection with Girton College. Much of it has been based upon a study of the original sources, but great help has been gained from modern writers, especially Friedländer. For the section on Asia Minor I am indebted mainly to Professor Ramsay's works on the subject, which he has made his own.

When so much has been written on a period, originality is difficult for those who cannot adduce fresh evidence. The general plan, however, and the concluding section, I can claim for the most part as my own. Also my own reading has furnished the references to the following authors :—Horace, Juvenal, Tacitus, Suetonius, the younger Pliny, Philo Judaeus, Dio Chrysostom, Plutarch, and Philostratus. The same may be said of the majority of references to Strabo, Ovid, Seneca, Martial, and the elder Pliny. A list of modern works consulted is prefixed to the essay.

I would venture to express my grateful thanks to the Syndics of the University Press for undertaking the publication of this book. I am also much indebted to Professor Ramsay both for reading part of the proofs and for kindly allowing me to adapt a map from his *Historical Commentary on the Epistle to the Galatians.* Lastly, I am glad to have this opportunity of acknowledging the kindness of the Rev. C. E. Graves, who has read all the proofs, and whose suggestions have been a constant help and encouragement.

C. A. J. S.

July, 1901.

TABLE OF CONTENTS.

MAPS.

The chief lines of Road in the Roman Empire.

Asia Minor, showing chief Roads in 1st Century A.D. etc.

available for download from www.cambridge.org/9781107635487

ERRATA.

Page 47, line 8 *for* Municipialis *read* Municipalis.
  ,,   94 *ad fin. for* Narbonnensis *read* Narbonensis.

LIST OF MODERN AUTHORITIES.

W. T. ARNOLD. Roman system of Provincial Administration.

BAUMEISTER. Various articles, Seewesen etc.
BECKER. Gallus.
BERGIER. Histoire des grands chemins de l'empire romain.
    3rd edition, 1728.
BUNBURY. History of Ancient Geography.
BURY. Student's Roman Empire.
   ,, History of the Later Roman Empire.

CONYBEARE and HOWSON. Life and Epistles of St Paul.
    1862.

FARRAR. Life and Work of St Paul.
FRIEDLÄNDER. Sittengeschichte Roms. 5th edition, 1881.

GIBBON. Decline and Fall of the Roman Empire.
GUHL and KONER. Life of the Greeks and Romans. 3rd
    edition, 1889.

HARDY. Pliny's Correspondence with Trajan.
HATCH. The early organization of the Christian Church.
HOGARTH. A Wandering Scholar in the Levant.

A. H. KEANE. Asia.

LANCIANI. Ancient Rome.
   ,, Pagan and Christian Rome.
LIGHTFOOT. Epistle to the Galatians.

MAHAFFY. The Greek World under Roman Sway.
MANNERT. Edition of the Peutinger Table.
MAYOR. Edition of Juvenal.
MERIVALE. History of the Romans under the Empire.
MIDDLETON. Remains of Ancient Rome.
MOMMSEN. History of Rome.
      „   Provinces of the Roman Empire.
      „   Römisches Staatsrecht.

PARTHEY and PINDER. Edition of the Itineraries.
PERROT. Exploration archéologique.
PERRY. Art. 'Viae' in last edition of Smith's Dict. of Antiquities.

RAMSAY. Historical Geography of Asia Minor.
      „   The Church in the Roman Empire.
      „   Cities and Bishoprics of Phrygia.
      „   St Paul the Traveller and the Roman Citizen.
      „   Impressions of Turkey during twelve years' wanderings.

SEYFFERT. Dictionary of Antiquities.
STERRETT. Epigraphical Journey through Asia Minor.

TORR. Ancient Ships.
TOZER. History of Ancient Geography.

Also the following collections of Inscriptions :—

BÖCKH. Corpus Inscriptionum Graecarum.

GRUTER. Inscriptiones Antiquae totius orbis Romani.

MOMMSEN. Corpus Inscriptionum Latinarum.

RUSHFORTH. Latin Historical Inscriptions illustrating the history of the early Empire.

CHAPTER I.

OBJECTS OF TRAVEL.

In the history of the early Church, as recorded *Rapid dif-* in the New Testament, there are two features which *fusion of Christi-* seem especially worthy of remark: the rapidity *anity in the first* with which Christian communities were formed, and *century* the constant intercourse maintained amongst them. A.D. Within thirty years after the Resurrection of Our Lord the Christian faith had been preached not only in the regions immediately adjoining Palestine, but in Asia Minor and Macedonia, Achaia and Illyricum, and even in Rome itself. The life of St Paul after his conversion is the life of one who for years was a constant traveller by land and sea, who in early manhood preached the Gospel at Damascus, and when old age was approaching looked forward to a journey into Spain. St Peter addresses his First Epistle to the strangers scattered through five provinces of Asia Minor, and in the concluding chapter sends them a message from the church at Babylon. No less do Pagan writers bear witness to the rapid diffusion of Christianity[1]. Pliny's correspondence with Trajan[2] shows that by

---

[1] Tac. *Ann.* xv. 44.   [2] Plin. *Epp. ad Trai.* 96 (97).

112 A.D. a province so insignificant as Bithynia
contained numerous Christians not only in the
cities but also in the villages and country.

*Inter-
course
between
Christian
com-
munities.*
The founders of these widely scattered communities realized the importance of intercommunication.
By personal visits, by letters, and by messengers
they sought to strengthen the ties which bound
them and their converts together into one Church.
The result is seen in the kindly feeling which
prompted the Christians of Antioch to send help
in time of famine to their brethren of Jerusalem,
and the Christians of Philippi to supply the neces-
sities of St Paul. Hospitality is one of the duties
expressly mentioned by St Paul in the Epistles to
Timothy and Titus as incumbent on bishops, while
St Peter and the author of the Epistle to the
Hebrews enjoin it on all Christians.

This rapid diffusion of a faith which could count
at first on little human aid, and this maintenance
of intercourse between its adherents, imply that the
means of communication in the first century after
Christ had reached a high stage of development.
It is the object of this essay to investigate the conditions of travel during that period; especially in
Asia Minor, where Christianity made some of its
earliest, though not most permanent conquests.

Before travelling can become a habit, men must
in the first place be supplied with motives strong
enough to overcome their shrinking from the un-
familiar; they must also have attained enough
mechanical skill to conquer the difficulties put by
Nature in the way of locomotion; and lastly they

must be assured that travel is at least tolerably free from risk. In the first centuries of the Roman Empire these conditions were fulfilled with a completeness never attained before, and never attained afterwards till quite modern times. The *Travel for* Roman Empire extended from the Atlantic to the *State pur-* Euphrates, from the German Ocean to the borders *poses.* of Ethiopia. It comprised within its boundaries nations differing as widely as possible in race, language, religion, and in political relations to the mistress-city. The problem of welding together this heterogeneous mass tested Roman energy and enterprise. Common subjection to Rome and worship of the emperor suggested the idea of unity; the material bond was found in the network of roads which connected the several provinces with Rome and facilitated the defence of the frontiers.

The system of provincial government as estab- *The* lished by Augustus could not have been carried *Imperial* on a year had not communication with Rome been *Post.* frequent and rapid. The sending out of proconsuls and legati, of financial agents and officials of various grades, to say nothing of the changes in the disposition of the troops and fleets, all necessitated an elaborate system of communication. Hence the establishment by Augustus of the Imperial Post, which according to Suetonius[1] was intended for the use of the Princeps, his servants and messengers, or of those to whom he granted a special permission. Between each of the stations or 'mansiones' there

---

[1] Suet. *Aug.* 49.

were in general about six 'mutationes' where relays of horses (*veredi*) were kept, also mules, vehicles and a number of public slaves. These arrangements were strictly reserved for imperial officials or for those who received a special passport called a 'diploma.' This consisted of two folding tablets inscribed with the name of the reigning emperor, the name of the person authorized to use the post, and the period for which the permit was available. Thus the younger Pliny feels obliged to inform Trajan that he has given a 'diploma' to his own wife, so that she might the more quickly pay a visit of condolence to a relative[1]. The emperor replies that he approves, seeing that the grace of the visit would be marred by long delay. From another letter of Trajan's[2] we learn that a stock of dated passports was sent by the emperor to each provincial governor, and that none might be used whose dates had expired. The death of an emperor rendered the 'diplomata' issued by him invalid, as is shown by a passage in Tacitus[3]. Coenus, a freedman of Nero's, spread a report that the Fourteenth Legion had defeated the Vitellians, who really had just gained a victory at Bedriacum : his object was that the 'diplomata' of Otho, which were disregarded, might regain their force.

Vehicu-latio. The horses and mules required for the Imperial Post were at first supplied free of charge by the neighbouring communities. This 'vehiculatio' was

[1] Plin. *Epp. ad Trai.* 120 and 121.   [2] Ibid. 46 (55).
[3] Tac. *Hist.* II. 54.

however transferred by Claudius to the fiscus, according to an inscription found on the site of Tegea[1] and dating from A.D. 49—50. This states that Claudius had long endeavoured to shift the burden not only from the 'coloniae' and 'municipia' of Italy but also from all the provinces and cities; yet he had found much difficulty in so doing. The old state of things revived under Nero[2], and became especially burdensome under Domitian. One of Nerva's most popular reforms was to transfer the cost of vehicles, etc. in Italy to the fiscus. His act is recorded in one of his first brasses, struck in A.D. 97, which shows two mules feeding, just liberated from their yokes: the legend is VEHI-CVLATIO · ITALIAE · REMISSA[3]. The provincials, however, were not exempted till the time of Severus Alexander, when the entire expense of the post— then called the *cursus publicus*—fell on the fiscus.

Of vital importance for the safety of the Empire was the communication between Rome and the armies on the frontier[4]. Mommsen holds that Augustus established a regular system of 'legionary centurions' who served as couriers, commissariat agents and warders. They belonged to the legions stationed in the provinces; when at Rome they were considered to be on detached duty and were called 'peregrini.' They lived on the Caelian Hill in the Castra Peregrinorum under the Princeps

---

[1] Rushforth, No. 82, *C.I.L.* iii. Suppl. 7251.
[2] Plut. *Galb.* 8.
[3] Middleton, *Remains of Ancient Rome*, Vol. II. p. 356.
[4] Ramsay, *St Paul the Traveller and the Roman Citizen*, p. 348.

Peregrinorum (Greek στρατοπεδάρχης). Naturally in course of time they became detested as government spies. In all probability the centurion who conducted St Paul and other prisoners to Rome belonged to this class.

Under the same head of travel for State purposes must be reckoned the frequent journeys of the emperors themselves. Suetonius says of Augustus[1] that he visited every province except Africa and Sardinia; these he had prepared to visit after the defeat of Sextus Pompeius but he was prevented by severe storms, and afterwards had neither the motive nor the opportunity. The principate of Tiberius was a complete contrast to his predecessor's in this respect: for the first two years he did not set foot outside Rome[2]. Between that time and his retirement to Capreae he never went further than Antium, though he often promised to visit the provinces and armies, and made elaborate preparations almost every year. At various points vehicles and provisions were collected and many vows were offered for his safe return; but in the end he found some excuse for remaining in Rome, and thus earned his nickname of Callippides, the man who ran hither and thither and never advanced a step. Gaius visited Germany and Gaul, besides meditating an invasion of Britain, which his successor Claudius carried out. Nero spent a year in Greece, while all three Flavian emperors took part in campaigns. Imperial caprice often disorganized traffic. Among

---

[1] Suet. *Aug.* 47.   [2] Suet. *Tib.* 38.

other mad freaks of Gaius we are told that when in Gaul he sold off by public auction his sisters' furniture, ornaments and slaves; delighted with the result he sent to Rome for the old court furniture; so large a number of beasts of burden and vehicles was required to transport it to Gaul that the bread supply of the city ran short, and several litigants lost their cases through inability to appear in time[1].

Domitian's journeys seem to have been especially dreaded. In the Panegyric on Trajan[2] Pliny exclaims :—" Now there is no disturbance over requisitioning vehicles, no haughtiness in receiving entertainment. The same food suffices for the emperor as for his suite. How different was the journeying of the other emperor in days not long past, if indeed that was a journey, not a devastation, when he carried off the goods of his hosts, when everything right and left was brought to rack and ruin, just as if those very barbarians from whom he was fleeing were falling upon the place."

Less often recorded, but still worthy of mention, are the journeys undertaken by the bearers of petitions or complimentary addresses to the emperor or to provincial governors. The Byzantines spent 12,000 sesterces (£96) yearly on the travelling expenses of a legatus bearing to Trajan a formal honorary decree; also 3000 sesterces (£24) on sending an envoy to salute the governor of Moesia. Pliny with the emperor's approval cut down these expenses, doubtless to the delight of the citizens[3].

---

[1] Suet. *Cal.* 39.   [2] Plin. *Pan.* 20.

[3] Plin. *ad Trai.* 43 (52) and 44 (53).

In spite of all the efforts of the government the
journey from the East to Rome had its perils; we
still have a marble on which the envoys sent from
Mehadia on the Danube engraved their thanks to
the Divinities of the Waters for having brought
them back safe and sound[1]. These complimentary
decrees formed part of the business transacted at
the annual meetings of the provincial concilia or
κοινά, which must have given rise to a good deal
of travelling[2]. Lastly, the 'appeal unto Caesar'
allowed to Roman citizens by the Lex Iulia de
Appellatione, brought many accused persons to the
capital. Besides the famous instance of St Paul,
we have a reference to the custom in Pliny's letter
to Trajan, which states that orders have been given
for those Christians who were Roman citizens to be
sent 'ad urbem[3].'

Commerce.   Next in importance among the motives for
travelling comes the hope of gain by trade. Rome
in the first century A.D. was the emporium for the
Mediterranean, indeed for the whole known world.
Both for her necessaries and for her luxuries she
depended mainly on foreign imports. The traffic
in corn between Rome and the provinces of Gaul,
Spain, Sardinia and Sicily, Africa and Egypt, was
regularly organized under the Praefectus Annonae.
Year by year the convoy from Alexandria was
eagerly awaited; a letter of Seneca's describes how
when the corn-fleet was sighted with its despatch

---

[1] Duruy, quoted by Bury, *Student's Roman Empire*, p. 442.
[2] Hardy, "Provincial Concilia," *Eng. Hist. Rev.* 1890.
[3] Plin. *Epp. ad Trai.* 96 (97).

boats (naves tabellariae), its escort of war galleys, and its topsails flying, all Puteoli streamed out to the harbour-moles. Among other imports were objects of luxury from the East, such as ivory, cotton, silk, pearls, gums and spices; manufactures, such as paper from Egypt, woollen dyed stuffs from Asia Minor, and the finest wines from Greece and the islands of the Aegean. To these must be added silver from the Spanish mines, wild animals for the sports of the amphitheatre, and marbles for the buildings which in a few decades utterly transformed the capital of the Empire. Rome had become a commercial as well as a military State; her traders were found not only in every province, but in the wild regions of the Marcomanni, in the far East, and even in the Irish Sea[1]. Eager pursuit of wealth is to Horace and to Seneca one of the marked features of the age. " A busy trader, you rush off to the farthest Indies, flying from poverty over sea, over crags, over fires[2]." "Another man," writes Seneca, "through his eagerness as a merchant is led to visit every land and every sea by the hope of gain[3]." The same author in a well-known denunciation of Roman habits writes as follows: " May the gods and goddesses bring ruin upon those whose luxury transcends the bounds of an Empire already perilously wide. They want to have their ostentatious kitchens supplied with game from the other side of the Phasis, and though Rome has not yet obtained satisfaction from the Parthians, are not ashamed to obtain birds from them: they

[1] Tac. *Agric.* 24; *Ann.* II. 62.   Plin. *H. N.* VI. 101, 173.
[2] Hor. *Epp.* I. 1. 45, 46.   [3] Sen. *De brev. vit.* 2.

bring together from all regions everything, known or unknown, to tempt their fastidious palate[1]."

Peace established. Closely connected with this wide-spread commerce were the peace and order ensured by Augustus and his successors. The last years of the Republic had seen wars with hardly a break, pirates making descents not only on the shores of the Aegean but on Sicily and even on Italy itself, brigands rendering traffic insecure within a few miles of Rome. Augustus by his vigorous administration made the 'Pax Romana' a reality, and for more than fifty years after his death peace continued with the exception of frontier wars. Greek though he was, Strabo was impressed as strongly as Horace or Vergil by the safety of life and property, the security for commerce and the advantages to civilization which arose from a centralized administration. "Never," he says, "have the Romans and their allies enjoyed such peace and prosperity as that conferred on them by Augustus Caesar, and now by his son and successor Tiberius[2]." Half a century later the elder Pliny speaks in the same strain of the "immensa Romanae pacis maiestas," and prays for the long continuance of that blessing which has been "little less than a new sun to the human race[3]."

Travelling for pleasure and health. This comparative immunity from danger enabled many other classes besides officials to indulge in travelling. The elder Pliny[4] remarks that mankind is ever eager to hear new things, and the younger

---

[1] Sen. *Cons. ad Helv.* 10, translated by A. Stewart.
[2] Strab. vi. 4. 2.   [3] Plin. *H. N.* xxvii. 1.
[4] Plin. *H. N.* xvii. 66.

Pliny speaks of Greece, Asia Minor and Egypt as places which every cultivated man must desire to see[1]. The account of Germanicus' journey given by Tacitus[2] is especially noteworthy from this point of view. After a stormy voyage over the Adriatic and Ionian Seas to Nicopolis, he spent a few days in repairing his ships and inspecting the relics of the battle of Actium. He then sailed round Cape Malea to Athens, where he was received with enthusiasm. Pursuing his course, he visited Euboea, Lesbos, Perinthus and Byzantium, "being desirous of acquaintance with ancient regions celebrated in history." On his return journey he was anxious to see the mysteries at Samothrace, but was prevented by contrary winds. After a visit to Ilium, the reputed cradle of the Roman race, he coasted along Asia and touched at Colophon to consult the oracle of the Clarian Apollo. The remainder of A.D. 18 was taken up with his expedition to Armenia and his open quarrel with Piso. Next year he set out for Egypt to study its antiquities. Sailing from Canopus up the Nile to the ruins of Thebes, he visited the statue of Memnon, the Pyramids, and the lake to hold the overflow of the Nile waters. Still further south he reached Elephantine and Syene, then the frontier cities of the province of Egypt.

In Italy itself too there was a great amount of travel, partly for pleasure, partly for health. Rome was deserted in the summer and early autumn owing to the heat and risk of fever; all who could, retired to

---

[1] Plin. *Epp.* VIII. 20 : cf. Hor. *Epp.* I. 11.

[2] Tac. *Ann.* II. 53.

their country seats or to the seaside resorts. During the hot weather Augustus, we are told, stayed on the shore or islands of Campania, or else at Lanuvium, Tibur, or Praeneste[1]. Nero spent much time at Baiae, where the season was at its height in March and April[2]. The fashionable Roman would spend his midsummer in cooler retreats, such as Tusculum, Tibur, Aricia, the Anio district or Mount Algidus[3]. Even those whose business detained them in the city would often spend their evenings in the country: this was the case with the younger Pliny, who had a villa at Laurentum, seventeen miles from Rome, and enjoyed travelling from one abode to another[4]. Few epigrams of Martial are more beautiful than that in which he describes the villa of his friend Apollinaris at Formiae[5]:

> "O temperatae dulce Formiae litus
> Vos, cum severi fugit oppidum Martis
> Et inquietas fessus exuit curas,
> Apollinaris omnibus locis praefert."

Life at Rome was burdensome at the best, with its numberless social duties and public shows, its frequent fires and its noisy crowds. Yet often men sought in their country seats not so much rest and quiet as relief from ennui and dissatisfaction. "This," says Seneca, "is the reason why men undertake aimless wanderings, travel along distant shores

---

[1] Suet. *Aug.* 72.   [2] Mart. x. 51.
[3] Mart. iv. 60.
[4] Plin. *Epp.* ii. 17, iii. 19.   Cf. Lanciani, *Ancient Rome* (The Roman Campagna).
[5] Mart. x. 30.

and at one time by sea, at another by land, try to
soothe that fickleness of disposition which is always
dissatisfied with the present. 'Now let us make for
Campania: now I am sick of rich cultivation: let us
see something of wild regions, let us thread the
passes of Bruttii and Lucania: yet amid this wilderness one wants something of beauty to relieve our
pampered eyes after so long dwelling on savage
wastes. Let us seek Tarentum with its famous
harbour, its mild winter climate and its district,
rich enough to support even the great hordes of
ancient times. Let us now return to town; our
ears have too long missed its shouts and noise: it
would be pleasant also to enjoy the sight of human
bloodshed.' Thus one journey succeeds another, and
one sight is changed for another[1]."

Of a higher stamp than these idle pleasure- *Travelling*
seekers were the numerous writers on antiquities, *for know-*
geographers, naturalists, and explorers. Such were *ledge.*
the two 'holy men' who, as Plutarch tells us, met
at Delphi from the very ends of the earth. Demetrius the grammarian was returning home out of
Britain to Tarsus, and Cleombrotus the Lacedaemonian had long been wandering in Egypt, reaching
even the country of the Troglodytes and voyaging
beyond the Red Sea. He had gone thither not for
trading purposes but through love of seeing and of
learning[2]. Chief among such travellers was Strabo
the geographer. It is true that in his day the limits
of geographical knowledge were small indeed as

---

[1] Sen. *De Tranq.* ch. 2, translated by Aubrey Stewart.
[2] Plut. *De defect. Orac., ad init.*

compared with modern times. In western Europe,
Spain, Gaul, the Atlantic coast and south-eastern
Britain were known with tolerable exactness; in
the north little was known beyond the Elbe and
the Danube: the information collected by Pytheas
was excluded by Strabo from his work as fabulous.
In Asia the lands on the further side of the Palus
Maeotis were still unexplored and the descriptions of Herodotus, like those of Pytheas, found
little credence. Pompeius however in his Syrian
campaign had traversed the region between the
Euxine and the Caspian, and an account of it had
been written by his friend and companion Theo-
phanes of Mytilene. But the Caspian was still
believed to communicate with the Northern Ocean,
and the Jaxartes was still the limit of discovery to
the east. With regard to India, the peninsula of
Hindostan was unknown, and the Ganges was
thought to flow into the Eastern Ocean beyond the
Red Sea. Still, between the time of Strabo and
that of the elder Pliny intercourse between Egypt
and India had greatly increased, and a fair knowledge was gained of the coast between the Indus
and the port of Nelcynda. In Africa nothing was
known by Strabo south of the Cinnamon country
and the territory of the Sembritae about the Upper
Nile, while in the more westerly regions no one had
penetrated south of the Garamantes[1].

Only a small portion even of this limited area
was known to Strabo from actual visits: his travels

---

[1] This section is summarized from Tozer's *Ancient Geography*.

were probably confined to Asia Minor, parts of Italy and Egypt, and a few places in Greece. But his comprehensive and laborious work shows how keen was the interest he took in the outward world. Geography was to him a term of wide significance; it included the history, antiquities and political condition of a country as well as its physical features. Hence the great value of his records, especially for Asia Minor, which he described largely from personal knowledge[1].

The encyclopaedic work of the elder Pliny, some fifty years later in date, shows the desire of the age for information. He was however a compiler rather than a traveller: the modern reader cannot help wishing that on his journeys he had been less industrious in taking notes from others and had made more observations of his own. Had he done this his *Natural History* would have been less full, but would certainly have gained in vividness. Yet with all its defects it is an invaluable work for the information given on exploration and commerce and for its ample statistical details.

Even more frequent was travel for the sake of education. "Are young men," says Epictetus, "to leave their homes only to hear a pseudo-philosopher repeat mere words, and cry out Oh! to him[2]?" There was an ample choice of places for study; besides Athens, Rome, and Alexandria, the three greatest, several towns in Asia Minor attracted students. The Syrian Antioch had been famous

Travel for education.

1 Ramsay, *Hist. Geog. of Asia Minor*, p. 73.
2 Epict. *Diss.* III. 21. 8.

in Cicero's time[1] for its men of learning; to Smyrna
came youths not only from the neighbouring districts, but from Greece, Assyria, Phoenicia and
Egypt. Of Tarsus Strabo[2] says that its schools of
philosophy surpassed even those of Alexandria and
Athens though few strangers visited them : however
the Tarsians visited other places of learning and in
many cases never came back. Teachers as well as
learners constantly travelled. Dio of Prusa when
bidden by the Delphic oracle to " go on as he was
doing till he came to the world's end " put on a
beggar's dress and wandered everywhere, "being taken
by some for a vagabond, by others for a beggar,
by others again for a philosopher[3]." Rhetors too
journeyed from place to place to deliver those
discourses in which " they talked at large on everything which was not practical and not instructive "
(Mommsen).

Needy persons[4] were often attracted to Rome by
the almost gratuitous distribution of corn, by the
frequent shows and largesses, or by the hope of dole
from some rich patron. Martial's epigrams give a
lively picture of the miseries that such new comers
often endured, living or rather starving in wretched
garrets, and tramping through cold or wet to pay
the duty visit which brought only a meagre dinner
in return. More than once he roundly advises his
friends not to come to Rome if they wish to gain a

---

[1] Cic. *pro Arch.* 3 § 4.   [2] Strab. p. 673.
[3] Dio Chrys. *Or.* xiii. 422 R.
[4] Cf. Epict. *Diss.* i. ch. 10. 'Against those who eagerly seek
preferment at Rome.'

livelihood by honest means. "If you are honest,"
he tells Sextus[1], "you may *possibly* keep alive," and
asks Fabianus what a man who is poor and truthful
can hope to find in the city[2]. Wiser was the
'esuritor Tuccius,' who came from Spain to find a
patron, but on hearing that no dole was to be had,
turned back from the Mulvian Bridge[3].

Among other classes of travellers may be men-   *Other*
tioned the physicians and quacks[4], the jugglers,   *travellers.*
conjurers and spell-mongers, the musicians and
athletes, on their way to fairs or the great festivals
which formed the serious business of many towns in
Greece and Asia Minor. Plutarch tries to console a
friend condemned to exile by telling him that he
can be present at the Eleusinian mysteries, at the
Dionysiac festival at Athens, at the Nemean games
of Argos, at the Pythian games of Delphi, and can
pass on and be a spectator of the Isthmian and
Corinthian games if he is fond of sight-seeing[5].
The mysteries of Eleusis and Samothrace, famous
temples, such as those of Artemis at Ephesus and of
the Great Mother at Comana Pontica, continued to
attract crowds of worshippers. The oracles, though
some were strangely silent, were still consulted, as
for instance by Titus, who after hearing of Galba's
death came from Corinth to the temple of Venus
at Paphos[6].

---

[1] Mart. iii. 38.   [2] Mart. iv. 5.
[3] Mart. iii. 14.
[4] Cf. Cic. *pro Cluent.* 24, L. Clodium pharmacopolam circum-
foraneum.
[5] Plut. *de exil.*   [6] Tac. *Hist.* ii. 2.

Temples were visited not only for worship, but for the recovery of health : they were in fact the ancient equivalents of our hospitals and medical schools. Chief among them were the temples of Aesculapius at Cos and at Epidaurus. Thither pilgrimages were made in the hope that as the sick folks slept in the precincts the god would appear and tell them the proper remedies. In a temple of Aesculapius at Aegae near Tarsus, Apollonius of Tyana spent some years of his boyhood : among the patients whom he is said to have met there was a young Assyrian, who however was for a long time too self-willed to benefit by the treatment he had come so far to seek[1]. Patients who had been cured often hung up in the temple votive-offerings, usually limbs or figures modelled in terra-cotta, of which great numbers have survived. Professor Lanciani says that he has been present at the discovery of no fewer than five deposits of votive-offerings, each marking the site of a place of pilgrimage. Perhaps the most interesting of those which he describes are the temples of Diana Nemorensis and of Juno at Veii. At the latter place a mass of ex-votos has accumulated under a cliff on the north side of a ridge connecting the fortress and the city. When excavations were made in 1889 four thousand objects were collected in a fortnight[2].

Health-seekers were often sent by their physicians to milder or more bracing climates as their case

<hr/>

[1] Philostrat. *Vit. Apoll.* I. 9.
[2] Lanciani, *Pagan and Christian Rome*, p. 59 *et seq.*

required[1]. An example is to be found in the letter
of the younger Pliny to Paulinus. Zosimus, Pliny's
freedman, had become seriously ill through overstrain
of his voice in reading aloud; his patron had sent
him to Egypt for a long stay with beneficial results.
Exertion however brought back a return of the
malady, and Pliny proposed to send him to Paulinus'
farm at Forum Iulii to get good milk and good air[2].

One more class of travellers remains to be *The Jews.*
mentioned, the Jews, whose wide dispersion is
attested both by literary evidence and by the
number of inscribed tombstones they have left[3].
Many of them came up periodically to the Feasts
at Jerusalem, as we read in the Gospels and the Acts
of the Apostles. Every year too the 'didrachma[4]'
was sent up by each Jew to the Temple, and the
conveyance of these sums from almost every part of
the known world led to a great amount of travel.
Thus Philo Judaeus writes of the Jews beyond the
Euphrates, "Every year the sacred messengers are
sent to convey large sums of gold and silver to the
Temple, which have been collected from all the
subordinate governments. They travel over rugged
and difficult and almost impassable roads, which
however they look upon as level and easy, inasmuch
as they serve to conduct them to piety[5]."

Such then are some of the most important classes
of travellers in the first century of our era. They

[1] Epict. *Diss.* III. 16. 2.
[2] Plin. *Epp.* v. 19.
[3] See the last vol. of *C. I. G.*
[4] S. Matt. xvii. 24.
[5] Phil. Jud. *On the Virtues and Offices of Ambassadors*, 31.

belong to all grades of society, from the Princeps to
the beggar, from the rich merchant to the strolling
actor. A frequented Roman road such as the Appian
or Flaminian must have presented an animated
appearance even on ordinary days, not to speak of
such occasions as the return of a popular emperor
like Trajan from a successful campaign. " When will
the day be," asks Martial[1], " for the Campus to be
thronged even to the trees, and for every window
to be bright with Roman matrons in festal garb?
When will be those halts to please the crowd, and
the whirlwind of dust raised by Caesar's suite?
When will all Rome stream out on the Flaminian
Way? When will the Moorish cavalry dash past in
their broidered tunics, and when will the shout of
the people rise, 'He comes'?"

Perhaps the crowds that flocked to a great city
cannot be better described than in a passage of
Seneca which deserves to be quoted in full[2]. He is
seeking to console his mother Helvia for his exile,
and argues that many men leave their homes of
their own accord. " 'It is unbearable,' say you, 'to
lose one's native land.' Look, I pray you, on these
vast crowds for whom all the countless roofs of
Rome can scarcely find shelter: the greater part of
those crowds have lost their native land: they have
flocked hither from their country-towns and colonies
and in fine from all parts of the world. Some have
been brought by ambition, some by the exigencies
of public office; some by being entrusted with

[1] Mart. x. 6.
[2] *Cons. ad Helv.* c. 6 (translated by A. Stewart).

embassies ; some by luxury which seeks a convenient spot rich in vices for its exercise ; some by their wish for a liberal education, others by a wish to see the public shows. Some have been led hither by friendship, some by industry, which finds here a wide field for the display of its powers. Some have brought their beauty for sale, some their eloquence; people of every kind assemble themselves together in Rome, which sets a high price both upon virtues and vices. Bid them all to be summoned to answer to their names, and ask each one from what home he has come ; you will find that the greater part of them have left their own abodes, and journeyed to a city which, though great and beauteous beyond all others, is nevertheless not their own. Then leave this city, which may be said to be the common property of all men, and visit all other towns : there is not one of them which does not number a large proportion of aliens among its inhabitants[1]."

[1] Cf. Dio Chrys. *Or.* viii. 277, 278 R for the motley collection of people at Corinth.

CHAPTER II.

THE MECHANISM OF TRAVEL.

THE foregoing evidence, which might be greatly amplified, proves that abundant motives for travel existed in the first century A.D. The next point to consider is what may be called the mechanism of travel, the routes followed, the construction and repair of roads, and the means of conveyance by *Authori-* land and sea. But before entering on this subject *ties on* something must be said as to the authorities on *the road-* the Roman road-system and their value. First in *system.* importance come the actual remains of roads, also milestones and inscriptions. Of course a milestone may often have been carried from the spot where it was originally set up: still, such stones are usually fairly heavy, and will therefore rarely be carried far. Next must be reckoned information from literary sources, especially the classical authors of the first century. But both earlier and later writers may be used in addition: references to Italian roads are found in Horace and Livy, and a description of an Alexandrian corn-ship is given by Lucian. In fact the topography, and therefore the road-system of a Roman province, cannot be satisfactorily settled without a full knowledge of its history as well as its physical features. For example, the Byzantine authorities have been largely used by Professor Ramsay in working out the Roman road-system of Asia Minor.

In the third place we have certain works which professedly deal with the imperial roads, viz. the Itinerary of Antoninus and the Peutinger Table. The Romans were nothing if not thorough ; every landowner was accustomed to have his property accurately measured, and the State was not behind-hand. Under the Republic the measurements of every acre of public land were registered under the care of the censors. According to the fourth-century writer Vegetius, generals used to be furnished with some kind of plan, so that the roads in the provinces were not only noted for them but actually depicted[1]. Julius Honorius says that Julius Caesar ordered a measurement of the whole Empire to be undertaken and that it was carried out in four divisions, north, south, east, and west, through a period of five-and-twenty years. Neither Strabo nor Pliny confirms this statement, but it is quite certain that measurements of some kind, mainly for financial purposes, were made under Augustus. The industry of Agrippa collected in the form of ' commentarii,' a number of statistics, referred to by later geographers as the Chorographia. By way of instructing and astonishing the multitude of Rome, an Orbis Pictus was engraved on the Portico of Octavia erected in the

---

[1] Veg. *De Re Milit.* III. 6. (Merivale, Vol. IV. p. 403.)

Campus Martius[1]; also a list of the chief places on the roads radiating from Rome was inscribed on the so-called Golden Milestone in the Forum. In all probability the Orbis Pictus and the Chorographia, corrected from time to time, formed the basis of the 'itineraria adnotata' and the 'itineraria picta.' The Antonine Itinerary is a specimen of the former class, the Peutinger Table of the latter. Private persons seem to have possessed copies: Mettius Pompusianus was put to death by Domitian on the charge of carrying about "depictum orbem terrae in membrana[2]."

The Antonine Itinerary probably dates from the reign of Diocletian. It is simply a list of the great roads of the Empire, some three hundred and seventy-two in all, with their lengths. For the first century its evidence must be used with caution. Errors in the spelling of names are frequent, and in many cases the roads given are not direct between two given points, but go along two sides of a triangle. Ancient maps represented the face of a country very imperfectly, and it is useless to expect accuracy from a document depending on them.

This remark applies with even greater force to the Peutinger Table. Its history has been a curious one. Compiled probably in the fourth century A.D. under Valentinian II (375—394) it was transcribed in the thirteenth century by a monk of Colmar. This copy was discovered in 1507 in a German monastery by Conrad Celtes, and bequeathed for

---

[1] Plin. *H. N.* iii. 3.   [2] Suet. *Dom.* 10.

publication to his friend Conrad Peutinger of Augs-
burg. But the multitude of errors he found deterred
Peutinger from fulfilling this request. The veteran
geographer Ortelius begged in vain for the honour
of the task, which was finally undertaken by Moretus
of Antwerp. The Table was printed in 1682 in a
posthumous edition of Velserus' works. In 1720
the original transcript was bought by Prince Eugene
of Savoy for a hundred ducats, and after his death
it passed to the Imperial Library of Vienna, where
it has since remained. The western part has been
lost; the remainder comprises all the ancient world
between the east coast of Britain and the limits of
Alexander's eastern conquests. The course of the
great roads is marked, and the distance given in
miles from station to station.

The principle on which the Table was drawn has
little in common with that of the modern map.
The section dealing with Asia Minor (as given in
Mannert's reproduction) begins with a horizontal
strip of sea, underneath which is a band about an
inch-and-a-half deep representing the region of the
Amazons and the Caucasus. Then comes a narrower
strip for the Pontus Euxinus, and underneath a
much wider one for the bulk of Asia Minor. Below
this is the Aegean Sea, and last of all is a strip
showing Egypt, the Nile Delta, the blazing beacon
of the Pharos, and a piece of information evidently
supplied by the monk of Colmar, "Desertum ubi
quadraginta annos erravͭt filij isͬt ducente Moyse."
The chief towns of Asia Minor are denoted by two
tiny penthouses side by side, e.g. Pergamus, Synnada

and Pessinus; once a fort of a very mediaeval
character is drawn with six towers and a high wall
all round. Needless to say no attention is paid
to the points of the compass, *e.g.* Pergamus and
Smyrna are almost on a horizontal line. The
draughtsman often fell into difficulties; for instance
he was compelled to draw the course and the mouth
of the Sangarius in two disconnected bits. The
spelling is erratic; Iuforbio and Euforbio are found
for Euphorbio, and even Duse pro Solympum for
Prusa pros (πρὸς) Olympum. In fact the student
who attempts to extract information from this
tantalizing document is tempted to re-echo the
words of Cluverius: "ingentis usus opus si barbarum
illud saeculum quo librariorum incredibili imperitia
incuriaque corrupta fuerunt, salva ad nos sanaque
transissent. Nunc inutile, manca, detorta, ac plurima
ex parte depravata, nil nisi meras tenebras geogra-
phiae antiquae ignaris offundunt[1]." Yet the Table
is of value as confirmatory evidence, and of interest
as the only Roman road map that has come down
to us.

Before this list of authorities is concluded a word
must be said as to the three silver cups in the form
of milestones, found in 1852 at the baths of Vicarello
on the Lake of Bracciano, and now in the Kircherian
Museum at Rome. Engraved on them is a list of
stations and distances between Gades and Rome.
They are of great value as being older than the
Antonine Itinerary and showing that a considerable
number of Spaniards must have come for health to

[1] Quoted by Bergier, Vol. I. Bk. III. Ch. 9.

the baths, and made thankofferings to the local
deity. Such itineraries served the purpose of the
modern guide-books. In the fourth century a name-
less pilgrim, who had journeyed from Bordeaux to
Jerusalem, recorded the distances, the 'mutationes'
and the 'mansiones' with brief notices on points
of interest[1]. For example, against the 'mutatio
Euripidis' he writes 'ibi positus est Euripides poeta,'
and to the 'civitas Pellae' adds 'unde fuit Alexander
Magnus Macedo.'

By the help of these authorities it is possible to
ascertain with tolerable accuracy the main lines of
communication in the first century. After this lapse
of time complete knowledge can scarcely be hoped
for, at any rate not without more systematic exploration than is likely to be attempted.

The primary aim of the road-system was to
connect the provinces with the capital. The great
public roads (also called military, consular and praetorian) extended into almost every part of the
Empire. Branching off from them were the private
or rural roads, constructed originally by private land-
owners who had the power of dedicating them to the
public use. Often they were subject to a right of way
in favour of the public or the owner of a particular
estate. Lastly there were the 'viae vicinales,' which
were village, district, or cross roads leading through
or towards a village : these were considered public or
private according as the expense of making them
had fallen on the State or on private persons. The

*Classifi-
cation of
roads.*

---

[1] See Wesseling, pp. 604—606.

private and cross roads have left no traces, as they would not probably be paved or provided with milestones[1]. The public roads, however, can be traced in every province though with varying certainty and fulness. They may be most easily classified according to the region which they connected with Rome.

Chief lines of communication.
1. South.
The list begins with the oldest, the 'queen of Roman roads,' the Appian Way, along which went the traffic between Rome and the South[2]. It was made in 312 B.C. by the Censor Appius Claudius Caecus from the Servian Porta Capena as far as Capua: later it was extended to Brundisium. Procopius, writing in the first half of the sixth century A.D., describes it as broad enough for two carriages to pass each other, and built of hard stones hewn smooth: these were fitted exactly together, without metal or connecting material, so that the whole seemed to have grown together notwithstanding the great traffic that had passed along it[3]. From Capua a road ran along the coast of Lucania and Bruttium to Rhegium, whence an hour-and-a-half's crossing brought the traveller to Messina. Thence he followed the Sicilian coast road past Himera, Panormus and Segesta to Lilybaeum. In another twenty-four hours he had crossed to Carthage. The

[1] The direction of such roads can of course be fixed when the position of a Roman villa is known. A villa would necessarily imply a road of some kind.

[2] The account of the main routes is mainly taken from Friedländer, Vol. II. p. 7 *et seq.*, who follows Stephan (*Verkehrsleben*), p. 101 *et seq.*

[3] Procop. *De Bell. Goth.* I. 14, quoted in Becker's *Gallus.*

great city destroyed by the brutal selfishness of the Republic had prospered after its restoration by Julius Caesar. Governed at first as a Phoenician city under sufetes, it soon obtained Italian organization and full rights of Roman citizenship. It rose to importance as the capital of the African province garrisoned by imperial troops, a distinction which it shared with Rome and Lugdunum alone among the cities of the West. Hence was exported the African corn, which amounted to one-third of the consumption of Rome. Among other articles of commerce which passed through it were slaves, especially the swift Numidian runners, horses, wild beasts for the shows, purple-dyed woollen stuffs, and leather goods[1].

In the sailing season the journey to Carthage could be more easily accomplished by taking ship from Ostia or Puteoli direct. With favourable winds the time required was about three days. From Carthage and the other great coast-cities of Africa and Numidia, such as Leptis, Hadrumetum and Hippo Regius, roads converged to Theveste, the headquarters of the Legion III, Augusta, and thence to the coast of the Lesser Syrtis. By the time of the Antonine Itinerary a road ran near the coast from Carthage to Tingi (Tangier) whence Spain could be reached in four hours. But probably the road dates mainly from the second century onward, when we have abundant evidence of activity in road-making. In Nero's time at any rate there was no road between

[1] Cf. Plin. *Epp.* VI. 34. The African panthers provided by Maximus for a gladiatorial show at Verona did not arrive in time through stormy weather.

Tingi and Caesarea, and all the traffic went by sea.
Hence the ease with which the Mauretanian hordes
crossed over to Hispania Baetica and menaced the
Roman subjects[1].

Eastward from Carthage a road led past the
Syrtes and Cyrene to Alexandria, the second city
of the Empire and the first commercial city of the
world[2]. It exported vast quantities of corn to
Rome, manufactured goods, such as paper, linen and
glass, spices from Arabia and Africa, granite from
Syene, and porphyry from the mountains above
Myos Hormos. Nor did Alexandria supply the neces-
sities and luxuries of the Empire alone: it sent
linens to Arabia, cloth of gold and glass to India:
its beads were bartered for African ivory, and its
corn for the tin of Britain. Alexandria owed much
to the imperial rule. Once as Augustus was sailing
past Puteoli he was greeted by the crew of a ship
hailing thence with shouts of gratitude "for life
itself, for liberty of trade, for freedom and fortune."
By way of acknowledgment the emperor gave his
suite forty aurei to be spent on the purchase of
Alexandrian wares. The Alexandrian Jew Philo
magnifies the benefactor "who did not only loosen
but utterly abolish the bonds in which the whole
habitable world was previously bound and weighed
down; who destroyed both the evident and unseen
wars which arose from the attacks of robbers; who
rendered the sea free from the vessels of pirates and
filled it with merchantmen[3]."

[1] Bury, p. 89 (*Student's Roman Empire*).
[2] Dio Chrys. *Or.* xxxii. 670 R. *et seq.*   [3] Phil. Jud. *De Leg.* 21.

Indeed the emperors had weighty reasons for developing the resources of Egypt and encouraging its trade. On Egyptian corn the overgrown population of Rome largely depended for its food, and the strongest emperor might quail before a famine-stricken mob. A proof of the attitude of the emperors towards Egypt is seen in the ordinance of Augustus forbidding any senator to visit it without permission, and in Vespasian's resolve to send subordinates to gain Italy, but secure Egypt himself. In the second place as the customs levied at Alexandria were very lucrative, the imperial policy aimed at securing direct communication with Arabia and India[1]. Under the weak rule of the later Lagidae the prosperity of Egypt had waned, and the control of the Red Sea had to a great extent passed to the Axomites and to the Arabians of Arabia Felix (Yemen). Departing from his usual policy Augustus sought to extend the Roman dominion in Arabia by a great expedition under Gallus, in which Strabo took part. Mismanagement 25 B.C. and disease combined to ruin the project, but twenty-five years later it was resumed. The young prince Gaius was sent to the East in the hope that he would, like Alexander's admiral Nearchus, make an exploring voyage from the mouth of the Euphrates along Arabia Felix. The untimely death of Gaius once more frustrated Augustus' hopes; all that was done was to send a small expedition to destroy Adane (Aden), the chief emporium on the south

---

[1] See Mommsen, *Provinces*, Vol. II. (Egypt).

Arabian coast. The Romans gained something thereby, but still had to reckon with the traders of Muza, who in their own ships sailed along the east coast of Africa and the west of India taking their own frankincense and the purple stuffs and gold embroideries of Alexandria, and bringing back spices, pepper and silks from the far East.

The Axomites on the other hand did not come into collision with Roman power. Their territory at the end of Nero's reign included the African coast from the site of Suakin to the Straits of Bab-el-mandeb. Later their sphere of influence extended to the coast of Arabia between the Roman and the Sabaean territories, and from the entrance of the Arabian Gulf to Cape Guardafui. The king contemporary with Vespasian was able and energetic and acquainted with Greek writing. His capital Adulis was the emporium of the Ethiopian trade, and he did much to secure freedom of communication with the Roman frontier both by land and sea.

Coming to the actual routes by which the Eastern traffic was carried on, we find that from Alexandria roads led on either side of the Nile past Coptos, Thebes and Syene to Hiera Sykaminos, on the frontier of Aethiopia. From Coptos roads led north-east to Myos Hormos on the Arabian Gulf, while a march of eleven days to the south-east led to Berenice, the port for the country of the Troglodytes. Both these desert roads were provided with stations and cisterns (*hydreumata*). Camels were employed and the journeys mostly made by night. At the time of Strabo's Egyptian visit a hundred and twenty ships sailed from Myos Hormos through the Arabian Gulf to India, a number which showed the impetus given to commerce by the imperial government.

For our knowledge of the communication between Egypt and India we are indebted chiefly to the elder Pliny and the author of the *Periplus Maris Erythraei*, a Greek trader living in Egypt during the Flavian era. Myos Hormos, as in Strabo's time, was the starting point of the Indian fleet, which was provided with archers as a defence against the poisoned arrows of the Arabian pirates. A voyage of thirty days past Adulis led to Ocelis and Cane on the southern coast of Arabia. Further east the promontory of Syagros (C. Fartak) was the point of departure for the direct voyage to India. This was first tried by Hippalus, a Greek of the post-Augustan period, who used the south-western monsoon henceforth called after him. The author of the *Periplus* shows a very fair knowledge of Western India from the mouth of the Indus to the Malabar coast. He mentions the large inlet Eirinon (Runn of Cutch), the bay to the south of Baraces (Gulf of Cutch), and the gulf (of Cambay), at the head of which was the seaport of Barygaza, the most famous emporium for perfumes, precious stones, ivory, muslin and silk. Further south were the ports of Musiris and Nelcynda; the latter was the seat of the trade in pepper, which was brought down to the coast by natives in canoes hollowed out of tree-trunks. Hippalus probably sailed from Arabia to Barygaza, but his successors established a regular line of traffic with Musiris and Nelcynda. The profits of this trade were enormous, the goods selling in the West for a hundred times their cost price[1].

The return voyage was made in December or January by the help of the wind called Vulturnus (S.S.E.) and of the Africus (S.W.) or Auster (S.) after entering the Red Sea. Under favourable circumstances the double journey took six or seven months, from the summer solstice to February. Indian imports, instead of going on to Alexandria, were sometimes landed at Leuce Come in Arabia and thence taken to Syria by way of Petra and Gaza. The sea-route however was found less costly and tedious.

With China no regular communication was established. The silk of the Seres, who lived northwest of Tibet, was chiefly brought by land to Syria, where it was worked up and then exported. Sailors however are known to have reached Further India, and the Romans at the beginning of the second century knew of the port of Cattigara, which was perhaps Hang-chow-foo at the mouth of the Yangtse-kiang.

Central African trade came chiefly north to Adulis; a long list of articles is given by Pliny, including, besides sphinxes and slaves, ivory, rhinoceros horns, hippopotamus hides, and tortoise-shell. The author of the *Periplus* knew the entrepôt Opone south of the promontory of Aromata (C. Guardafui), and the island of Menuthias, probably Pemba or Zanzibar. The coast-line further south

[1] Cf. Dio Chrys. *Or.* xxxv. 72 R. Vol. II.

was beyond his knowledge: from Menuthias he
thought it trended sharply to the west.

Communication between Rome and the East 2. *East.*
likewise began by the Appian Way. From Capua
there was a choice of routes to Brundisium; the
carriage road led through Venusia to Tarentum, the
bridle-road through Beneventum. From Brundisium
a voyage of some twenty-four hours brought the
traveller to Dyrrachium or Aulon, the termini of
the great Egnatian highway to the East. This led
through Illyria into Macedonia, passing Edessa,
Pella and Thessalonica, then along the neck of
Chalcidice to Thrace, and so to Byzantium. Among
its important branches were the roads down the
east and west of Greece meeting at Athens, and
the road from Aphrodisias to Calliupolis (Gallipoli)
in the Thracian Chersonese. A crossing of an hour
led to Lampsacus, whence the route lay across Asia
Minor to the Syrian Antioch. Here it met the
roads from the Euphrates and from Alexandria.
An alternative route was from Byzantium across
the Bosporus to Chalcedon and thence to Tarsus
and Antioch, by way of Nicomedia, Nicaea and
Ancyra. That this second route was much used is
proved by Trajan's letter to Pliny[1] mentioning the
military assistance given to the magistrates of
Byzantium as being a great city where a number
of strangers land.

In the first century A.D. Syria was the great
rival of Egypt in trade and manufacture. Agriculture too was in a thriving state; a good portion

[1] Plin. *Epp. ad Trai.* 77 (81).

of what is now called desert is rather, says Mommsen[1],
"the laying waste of the blessed labour of better
times." But important as the corn, wine and oil of
Syria were, its manufactures were more important
still. The purple-dyed stuffs and silks of Tyre and
Berytus, the glass of Sidon, and the fine linen of
some half-dozen Syrian towns were exported all over
the world. In spite of the development of the
Egyptian route for Arabian and Indian imports,
Syria maintained its connection with the East by
the caravan routes. One of these ran from Antioch
to Zeugma, where was the bridge of boats over the
Euphrates. Others led from Apamea, Emesa and
Damascus to Palmyra, whence a desert route lay to
the Euphrates at Sura opposite Nicephorium. The
Palmyrenes by way of return for semi-independence
seem to have guarded the crossing of the Euphrates
at Sura, the desert road up to their own city, and
possibly a part of the road west to Damascus.

The importance of Syrian commerce is attested
by the numerous records extant of the factories
throughout the Empire At Puteoli were settled
merchants from Berytus and Tyre, the latter receiving a subvention from their mother-city for
religious purposes. Syrians have also left records
of settlement at Malaga, and Gazaeans at Portus,
and we have a dedication made to L. Calpurnius
Capitolinus by the merchants trading in Alexandria,
Asia and Syria[2]. These busy traders were successors,
with happier fate, of the Syrian whom Theocritus

---

[1] *Provinces*, Vol. II. p. 136.

[2] See *C. I. L.* x. 1797; *C. I. G.* 5853, 5892.

had mourned; "Unhappy Cleonicus, thou wert eager to win rich Thasus, from Coele-Syria sailing with thy merchandise—with thy merchandise, O Cleonicus at the setting of the Pleiades thou didst cross the sea—and didst sink with the sinking Pleiades[1]."

Of less importance commercially but greater in a military point of view were the roads to the imperial provinces of the North and West. The chief Northern road was the Via Flaminia, made by C. Flaminius the censor from Rome to Ariminum, and continued by M. Aemilius Lepidus to Placentia, and ultimately to Mediolanum. At Placentia it was crossed by the Postumian road from Genua by way of Dertona to Verona and Aquileia. This road some thirty years later (109 B.C.) was directly connected with Rome by the Via Aemilia Scauri between Luna and Genua.

3. *North.*
220 B.C.
187 B.C.
148 B.C.

From Mediolanum branched several routes leading to Gaul, Germany, Rhaetia and Noricum. Past Placentia the road to Gaul lay through Augusta Taurinorum (Turin) north to Eporedia (Ivrea) and Augusta Praetoria (Aosta), which commanded two great Alpine routes. The southern crossed the Graian Alps (Little St Bernard) and led to the upper waters of the Isara and to Grenoble, thence to the Rhone at Vienna and north to Lugdunum. According to Strabo[2] this route was for the most part fit for wheeled traffic. In the wars of 69-71 A.D. it was often traversed, as for instance by the Four-

---

[1] Theocr. *Epig.* 9 (A. Lang's translation).
[2] Strab. p. 208.

teenth Legion[1] which Vitellius sent back to Britain
in 70 A.D. and by Cerealis and Annius[2] in the
campaign against Civilis. A second Alpine route
lay over the Cottian Alps (Mont Genèvre) to the
Druentia and Arelate : this was used by Valens the
general of Vitellius in 69[3]. Yet a third was the
direct but difficult pass from Augusta over the
Pennine Alps (Great St Bernard), down the Rhone
valley to the Lake of Geneva, then through Helvetia
and across the Jura till the Rhine was struck at
Augusta Rauracorum (above Bâle). Following the
course of the Rhine the road ran north to Argento-
ratum (Strasburg), Noviomagus (Speyer), Borbito-
magus (Worms) and thence to Moguntiacum (Mainz);
nor did it stop here, but trending slightly to the
north-west it passed Colonia Agrippina, Novesium
and Vetera, on to Lugdunum Batavorum (Leyden) at
the mouth of the Rhine.

These Alpine routes had been developed in the
Republican period, though often unsafe through the
attacks of mountain-tribes. Those that remain to
be described date from the extension of the northern
frontier of Italy and the organization of Rhaetia and
Noricum by Augustus and his step-sons. The starting
point for the connection with Rhaetia was Verona,
thence up the Athesis valley (Adige) the road lay
across the Brenner to Augusta Vindelicorum (Augs-
burg). This 'Via Augusta' was made in 15 B.C. by
the elder Drusus after the conquest of Rhaetia.
Thirty-two years later it was restored by Claudius

[1] Tac. *Hist.* II. 66.   [2] Ibid. IV. 68.
[3] Ibid. I. 61.

and renamed as the Via Claudia Augusta. Near
Feltre (Feltria) a milestone has been found stating
that Claudius as censor had restored from Altinum
to the Danube the road made by Drusus after
the opening of the Alps. Another stone has been
found near Meran. Some of the Roman roads in
Rhaetia are used to the present day, and are less liable
than the modern ones to destruction by floods[1].
The communications with Rhaetia were completed
by a road over the Splügen to Brigantia, north-east
to Augusta Vindelicorum and west to Vindonissa
(Bâle).

For the passes over the Julian Alps the starting
point was Aquileia, reached from Verona by the Via
Postumia or from Ariminum by road to Ravenna,
thence by boat over the 'Seven Seas' at the mouth
of the Padus and by road again from Altinum. From
Aquileia important roads diverged in three directions.
The first ran north-west through the Carnic Alps
and Noricum to Veldidena (Wilden) where it merged
in the Via Claudia Augusta. To the north-east the
old amber[2] trade-route led over the Julian Alps into
Pannonia past Aemona (Laybach), Poetovio, Savaria,
to Carnuntum and the Danube. Pliny mentions
that in Nero's time a Roman knight was sent by
the manager of a gladiatorial show to get amber.
He brought back such vast quantities from the bar-

[1] Friedländer, quoting from Planta, *Das alte Rätien.*
[2] Cf. Tac. *Germ.* 45. The Aestyi "on the right shore of the
Suevic Sea" collected amber, for which they had no use themselves,
and received with astonishment the large sums paid for the shape-
less masses.

barians, of North Germany that it was used for knots
on the netting that kept the beasts from the podium,
as well as for other decorations. Apparently he
reached the Baltic coast where the amber was found,
and calculated the distance from Carnuntum to be
six hundred miles. Along the Danube roads led
west to Vindobona and east to Aquincum, parallel
to the great 'Limes Rhaeticus,' which reaching its
final form under Hadrian extended from the junction
of the Danube and the Alcimona[1] (Altmühl) to
Lauriacum (Lorch), the starting point of the 'Limes
Germanicus.' Here may be mentioned too the roads
made by Vespasian in the Agri Decumates between
Germany and Vindelicia. The third road from
Aquileia led east through Siscia and Sirmium to
Viminacium, up the Morava valley to Naissus, then
through the Balkan passes to Serdica and Philippo-
polis to Byzantium. This was laid out immediately
after the annexation of Thrace in 46 A.D. and under
Nero[2] was furnished with resting-places (*tabernae*)
for ordinary soldiers and travellers, as well as
'praetoria' for officials.

4. *West.* Communication with the West was afforded
partly by the Alpine routes already described, but the
easier way was by the Via Aurelia from Rome past
Centumcellae (Città Vecchia) to Pisae and Luna to
Genua, thence by the Via Domitia along the Ligurian
coast to Massilia and Arelate. Still following the
coast-line, the road, now the Via Augusta, was continued to Narbo and over the Pyrenees to Tarraco,

[1] Bury, *Student's Roman Empire*, p. 405. [2] *C. I. L.* III. 6123.

thence across the Iberus through Valentia to the
mouth of the Sucro. It then turned inland over
the watershed of the Baetis, through Corduba and
Hispalis to Gades. In the first period of the Empire
much was done to improve communication in Spain,
as is evident from the number of milestones and
other inscriptions existing.

The same may be said of the roads in Gaul laid
out under the supervision of Agrippa with Lugdunum
as their centre. Thence diverged the southern route
to Arelate along the Rhone, and the western into
Aquitania through the Arverni and Augustoritum
(Limoges). Northwards the route lay up the Arar
valley to Cabillonum, whence communication with
the Rhine was afforded by a road up the Dubis
valley striking ultimately into that from the Pennine
pass. From Cabillonum Northern Gaul was reached
by way of Augustodunum (Autun), Durocortorum
(Rheims), Samarobriva (Amiens) to Gesoriacum
(Boulogne) the port for Britain.

By the date of the Antonine Itinerary the road-
system in Britain was very complete. Even in the
first century all the more important stations were
connected by roads radiating from Camalodunum
and Londinium. The chief were Watling Street
leading to Uriconium (Wroxeter) and Isca (Caerleon),
Ermine Street from Londinium to Camalodunum,
Lindum and Eboracum. A continuation of Watling
Street connected Londinium with the coast at
Rutupiae (Richborough), while the Fosse Way ran
right across the country from Isca (Exeter) to
Lindum.

An account of the great lines of communication would be incomplete without some mention of the customs-duties levied at various points on them. The 'portoria' were strictly levied at the frontiers, all imported wares paying duty, while some wares, iron especially, were forbidden to be exported. We know of nine specially organized taxation provinces; thus Asia formed one, Bithynia, Paphlagonia and Pontus another, and so forth[1]. The amount of duty was usually $2\frac{1}{2}$ per cent., but all Arabian and Indian goods had to pay 25 per cent. on being landed at any Red Sea harbour. Ethiopian goods paid duty at Syene: Egyptian exports paid at Schedia near Alexandria or at some other of the Nile mouths. The strictness with which dues were levied is illustrated by a chance allusion in Plutarch's essay on Curiosity. "We are not vexed," he writes, "with the custom-house officers if they levy tolls on goods bonâ fide imported, but only when they seek for contraband articles and rip up bags and packages; and yet

[1] These taxation provinces were:—

1. Sicily, duty of $5\,^0/_0$.
2. Spanish provinces, duty of $2\,^0/_0$.
3. Gallia Narb., duty of $2\frac{1}{2}\,^0/_0$.
4. The three Gauls, duty of $2\frac{1}{2}\,^0/_0$.
   (5 custom-houses known.)
5. Britain, duty of $2\frac{1}{2}\,^0/_0$ probably.
6. Moesia, Ripa, Thracia, Pannonia, Dalmatia, Noricum, duty of $2\frac{1}{2}\,^0/_0$.
7. Asia, duty of $2\frac{1}{2}\,^0/_0$.
8. Bithynia &c., duty of $2\frac{1}{2}\,^0/_0$.
9. Egypt.

(From Arnold, *Roman System of Provincial Administration*, based on Marquardt.)

the law allows them to do so and it is injurious to them not to do so."

Such is the outline of the road-system in the Empire, extending from the northern frontier of Britain to the borders of Ethiopia a thousand miles away, and to an even greater distance measured from east to west. A calculation has been made by Stephan of the length of a circular tour as follows:—from Alexandria to Carthage, Gades, Lugdunum, Gesoriacum, across to Londinium and the frontier of Britain on the north, back to Lugdunum Batavorum, Moguntiacum, Mediolanum, Aquileia, Byzantium, thence to Antioch and back to Alexandria. The total length he makes to be 1824 miles, of which all but about 180 miles could be traversed by Imperial roads.

CHAPTER III.

COMMUNICATION BY LAND.

Making of roads. THE next point to consider is the construction of this vast network of communications. A Roman road was intended to last; planned with utter disregard of expense and labour it was indeed 'fortified' rather than made[1]. Straightness and uniformity of level wherever possible were secured, no matter the difficulty of aqueducts or tunnels[2]. Thus the Via Appia is built on solid masonry through the valley of Aricia, and in the time of Augustus a tunnel, still in use, was cut to a length of half-a-mile out of the solid rock. Vitruvius, the writer on architecture in the Augustan period, gives full details as to making pavement; the process is also described by Statius in the poem[3] which celebrates the paving of the Via Domitiana from Sinuessa to Puteoli. The poet rejoices that the muddiness caused by the inundations of the Vulturnus is now removed, and that a

[1] In inscriptions the phrase for paving a road is silice sternere, elsewhere 'munire.'
[2] Cf. Middleton, *Remains of Ancient Rome*, Vol. II. p. 353.
[3] *Silv.* IV. 3.

journey which formerly took the whole day was
accomplished in under two hours:

> "At nunc quae solidum diem terebat
>   horarum via facta vix duarum."

He then goes on to describe the marking out of the
road by digging two parallel ditches (*sulci* or *fossae*)
within which the bed was first excavated (*gremium*).
The width between the trenches varied with the
importance of the road. On the Appian and
Flaminian Ways it was from 13 to 15 feet, while
the road up the Alban Mount to the Temple of
Jupiter Latiaris measured only 8. If a firm bed
for the pavement or dorsum could not be otherwise
obtained, wooden piles (*fistucationes*) were driven
in. Then came the work of filling in, first with the
'statumen,' stones as large as the hand could grasp,
then with the rubble (*rudus*), a mixture of stones
and lime about nine inches thick, well rammed down
with wooden beetles; above this came the 'nucleus,'
a six-inch layer of pounded pottery or burnt brick
mixed with lime. Lastly was laid the pavimentum
itself, usually polygonal blocks of lava (*silex*) most
carefully jointed together[1]. In the Forum at Rome
a fragment of old road still remains, but in most
places the blocks have been relaid in later times.

At the sides of the lava paving were kerbs of
tufa, peperino or travertine (*crepidines*). On one of
these Marius sat when "an exile among the ruins of
Carthage[2]." They were the favourite resting-places

---

[1] Cf. Tibull. i. 7. 60, apta iungitur arte silex.

[2] Sen. *Rhet. Contr.* 17 § 6, p. 198, quoted by Mayor, *Juv.* ii.
p. 150.

of beggars, as we learn from Juvenal, who asks the
poor client if he can find no vacant kerb-stone or
bridge rather than endure the meanness of a rich
patron[1]. The side-paths or 'margines' seem to
have been laid with gravel outside Rome, and inside
with rectangular slabs of hard stone (*saxum quad-
ratum*). The centre of the road was raised to let
the water run off, and cloacae were formed along
both sides with pipes at intervals. According to
Plutarch, horseblocks were placed here and there
along the Italian roads by C. Gracchus for the convenience of riders. Gracchus also paid much
attention to the erection of milestones, though it
is scarcely likely that none had been put up before,
as Plutarch seems to imply. The total expense
of a mile of Roman road has been calculated by
Friedländer as 100,000 sesterces or about £800 of
our money.

This elaborate system of paving was adopted
from the Carthaginians[2]. By the end of the Republic
it had been so fully carried out in Italy that there
were at least eleven important roads radiating from
Rome. In the provinces comparatively little had
been done, but Polybius mentions a road in the
Narbonensis, and Cicero the repair of the Via
Domitia by the lieutenants of M. Fonteius[3].
Further, the Via Egnatia was constructed after
the revolt of Macedonia in 149 B.C.

During this period the care of the roads was a

---

[1] Juv. v. 8.   [2] Isidore, Lib. 15, quoted by Bergier, Bk i.
[3] Cic. *pro M. Font.* c. 4.

duty of the censors[1], with whom the aediles were often *Repair of*
associated. They were superseded by a board of *roads.*
four commissioners for roads inside the city and of
two for those outside it, an arrangement which
shows the comparative insignificance as yet of the
provincial highways. The date of this change is
unknown, but it is first mentioned in the *Lex Iulia
Municipialis* of 45 B.C.[2] These commissioners
formed part of the body known as the viginti
sexviri, reduced by Augustus to the vigintiviri.
Already, however, curators had been sometimes appointed for some of the great roads. Julius Caesar
had been curator of the Appian Way: the care of
the Flaminian had been entrusted to Thermus, a
friend of Cicero's[3]. Augustus made the office
permanent, and put the holders on a level with
the ordinary magistrates. Under them were contractors (*mancipes*) and a staff of workmen. Com-
plaints against these contractors for fraud seem to
have been frequent[5]. The actual makers of the
road, besides skilled workmen, civil and military[6],

[1] Cf. Liv. IX. 29, IX. 43, X. 23. Epit. XX., XII. 27. Strabo, p. 217.
[2] See Mommsen, *Staatsrecht*, Vol. II. p. 588, p. 50 *et seq.*
quominus aed(iles) et IIIIvir(ei) vieis in urbem purgandeis,
IIvir(ei) vieis extra propiusve urbem Rom(am) passus [M] purgandeis queiquomque erunt vias publicas curent eiusque rei
potestatem habeant ita utei legibus pl(ebei) sc(itis) s(enatus)
c(onsultus) oportet oportebit, cum h(ac) l(ege) n(ihil) r(ogatur).

p. 69, quorum locorum quoiusque porticus aedilium eorum-
ve mag(istratuum) quei vieis loceisque publiceis u(rbis) R(omae)
propiusve u(rbem) R(omam) p(assus) M purgandeis praerunt,
legibus procuratis erit.

[3] Cic. *ad Att.* I. 1, § 2.   [4] Dio Cass. 59. 15.
[5] See Tac. *Ann.* III. 31.   [6] Ibid. I. 35.

were in many cases the provincials and condemned
criminals. Road-making is one of the hardships
mentioned by the chief Galgacus in his speech
before the battle of the Graupian Mount[1]. Criminals
imprisoned in Italy were by Nero's orders conveyed
to Lake Avernus for the construction of his projected
canal to Ostia; in fact some were condemned expressly for the work[2]. Trajan mentions road-making
as one of the occupations 'nearly penal' and fit for
criminals who had eluded punishment[3]. Gaius,
among other enormities, condemned men of good
station to the mines, to the making of roads, or to
the wild beasts[4].

Expense of maintaining roads.

Under the Empire the expense of making and
maintaining roads in Italy fell theoretically on the
aerarium, those outside were kept up by the fiscus.
In practice the two funds were amalgamated whenever the aerarium was empty. Roads in Rome and
doubtless in other cities were paved by the owners
of property. The viae vicinales were kept up by
the local authorities called 'magistri pagorum,' who
levied a kind of parish rate[5]. Augustus spent much
of his private means on the roads[6], even melting
down his silver presentation statues. His muni-
ficence is attested by the repair of the Flaminian
Road; as a memorial a triumphal arch was set up at
Ariminum[7]. At the same time (17 B.C.) an aureus
was struck "showing on the reverse part of the Via

[1] Tac. *Agric.* ch. 31.   [2] Suet. *Ner.* 31.
[3] Plin. *Epp. ad Trai.* 32 (41).   [4] Suet. *Cal.* 27.
[5] Sic. Flacc. *De Cond. Agr.* ed Goes, p. 9, quoted by Middleton.
[6] Dio Cass. 53.   [7] Gruter, p. 149, No. 2.

Flaminia, carried over a bridge, and surmounted by *Activity of the emperors in road-making.* a triumphal arch on which was a statue of the emperor, in a biga, crowned by Victory. The legend is QVOD·VIAE·MVNitae·SVNT " (Middleton). Another coin of Augustus struck in gold and silver states that he had given from his privy purse to the aerarium for the repair of the roads. He was heartily seconded in his efforts by his son-in-law Agrippa, who when aedile in 33 had spent large sums in paving the streets of Rome. Many contributions too were received from men who had received triumphal ornaments and a share in the spoil[1] from the enemy. Not only Italy, but the provinces, especially Gaul, Rhaetia, Noricum and Spain owed the beginning or the development of their roads to Augustus. This side of his work of reorganization is therefore fitly commemorated in the *Monumentum Ancyranum*[2] : " In my seventh consulship I paved the Flaminian Way from the city to Ariminum, and repaired all the bridges save the Mulvian and Minucian[3]."

Under Tiberius we find much evidence of activity in the same direction in Dalmatia, Moesia, Gaul and Spain[4]. An instance of his practical turn is given by Suetonius: he advised that the inhabitants of Trebia might be allowed to spend on a new road the

---

[1] *pecunia manubialis.*   [2] § 20.

[3] Cf. an inscription at Emerita in Spain (Grut. p. 149) which states that " Augustus after pacifying the world by land and sea, closing the Temple of Janus, and benefiting the Roman people by salutary laws, had widened and repaired the road (*sc.* passing Emerita) and extended it to Gades."

[4] See *C. I. L.* III. 3198, 3201, 1698. Rushforth, Nos. 88, 89. Grut. 153. 5 and 7.   *C. I. L.* v. 698, vv. 8—10.

sum bequeathed for a new theatre. The senate
however disagreed with him, and decided that the
testator's wishes should be respected[1]. Gaius, as
might be expected, did not interest himself in anything so commonplace and useful as a road, but his
successor Claudius resumed the policy of Augustus.
His repair of the Via Augusta over the Rhaetian
Alps has been mentioned in another connection[2] :
Pliny the elder speaks with approval of the roads he
hewed out between the mountains and the bridges
he constructed at enormous expense[3]. Nero's reign,
at least the later part, was a repetition of that of
Gaius. Still we find that besides the above-
mentioned improvements in the Thracian roads,
milestones bearing his name were set up at Errea
and Cordova[4]. Of Vespasian's work there are many
traces, especially in Spain; for example he restored
at his own expense the road from Coppara to
Emerita[5]. Aurelius Victor speaks of the excellent
roads he constructed throughout the Roman dominion, notably a tunnel 200 paces in length cut
through the Apennines on the Flaminian Road near
the modern Furlo. So wonderful was the work that
it received a special name, the Pertusa Petra ; the
inscription on the arch records that Vespasian had

---

[1] Suet. *Tib.* 31.

[2] *C. I. L.* III. pt 1, p. 61, No. 346, date 59/8 A.D.

[3] Cf. 152. 9; Grut. 153. 9.

[4] Grut. 154. 1, 2. Bergier, Vol. I. pp. 50, 51. Cf. *C. I. L.* III.
pt 1, p. 61, No. 346.

[5] Grut. 154. 3. Cf. *C. I. L.* III. pt 1, p. 88, No. 470,
A.D. 75.

acted in the capacity of censor[1]. Again, a senatus
consultum is extant which was passed in gratitude
for the money he spent on restoring the roads of the
city "which through the neglect of former times had
fallen into disrepair[2]." Titus in his brief reign seems
to have followed his father's policy: a milestone of
his remains in which the affection borne to him is
commemorated in the words *Generis Humani Amor
et Desiderium*[3]. Domitian too was a great road-
maker[4]: the Via Domitiana celebrated by Statius
was but one of his undertakings. A milestone of
his records that he had ordered the completion of
the road planned by his father and left unfinished
through the knavery of the contractors: they were
now severely punished and disabled from holding
public office again[5].

But perhaps the emperor who, after Augustus,
did most for communications was Trajan: his
harbour works will be described later, but his road-
making is equally important. A description of it
comes from a somewhat unlikely quarter. Galen in
his *Method of Medicine* compares the works of his
great predecessor Hippocrates to roads that need
improvement and cleaning. He goes on to say that
Trajan paved and embanked the roads in Italy that
had become damp and muddy, cleaned those that
were overgrown with weeds and thorns, and carried
bridges over unfordable rivers, besides making short
cuts and gentler ascents wherever possible[6]. Among

[1] Grut. 149. 7.   [2] Ibid. 243. 2.   [3] Ibid. 155. 3.
[4] C. I. L. III. 1, p. 57, Nos. 312, 318.   [5] Grut. p. 155.
[6] Galen, *Meth. Med.* Bk 9 ; cf. Grut. 151. 2.

his most important undertakings was the draining of the Pontine marshes and the continuation of the Via Appia from Forum Appii to the Temple of Feronia near Tarracina. Before this the Via Appia had made a *détour* to avoid the marshes, and travellers to save time used to cross by night in barges, as Maecenas and Horace did on their journey to Brundisium[1].

Road-making by private persons.   Such benefactions as those above described came from private persons as well as from the emperors. In honour of Augustus seven citizens of Falerii, holding the office of Augustales, paved the Via Augusta from the Via Annia outside the gate to the Temple of Ceres[2]. So too a physician, once a slave, leaves 307,000 sesterces to be spent for the public good on making roads. Lacer at Alcantara built a stone bridge and inscribed it with a dedication in elegiacs to Trajan. So too the Aquiflavienses dedicated to the same emperor a bridge made at their own cost. A similar act of generosity is recorded four or five miles from Ephesus on the road to Tralles[3]: the inscription in Greek and Latin on the remains of an aqueduct states that Sextilius and his wife and family have erected a bridge at their own expense in honour of the Ephesian Diana, Augustus, Tiberius and the city of Ephesus. Often the official curators themselves would defray part of the necessary charges; thus we find that a certain

[1] Hor. *Sat.* i. 5.   Strab. v. 232.

[2] Panvini, *In urbe Rom.*, Bergier, p. 88, Vol. i.   Bergier *ad loc. cit.*

[3] *C. I. L.* iii. 1, p. 81.

L. Appuleius "duumvir, curator viarum sternen-
darum" made 10,000 feet of road with his own
purse[1]. Such liberality was often rewarded with
honorary distinctions; the senate, for instance, with
Trajan's consent, conferred the triumphal ornaments
on certain officers who had acted as commissioners
of roads[2].

In order to complete the subject of road-making *Bridges.*
something must be said of the bridges in Rome and
the provinces. Most is known of course about those
across the Tiber. In the first century A.D. they
numbered at least eight. By far the oldest was the
Pons Sublicius, so called from the 'sublicae' or
wooden beams composing it. Only wood was used
for repairs, a custom originating in the legend that
Rome had been saved from Lars Porsenna and the
Tarquins by the cutting down of the bridge. The
real reason had been forgotten, viz. the belief that
to erect a bridge was to deprive the river-god of the
victims who would otherwise have been drowned in
trying to cross. A compromise between piety and
convenience was found by making a slight structure
which was less likely to offend the god than solid
masonry. In 69 A.D. it was carried away by a
sudden inundation of the Tiber: the site is not
certain but probably was near the Forum Boarium.

The first stone bridge in Rome was the Pons
Aemilius, begun in 179 B.C. by M. Aemilius Lepidus,
and finished in 142 B.C. by Scipio Nasica, the
adversary of Tiberius Gracchus, and L. Mummius,

---

[1] Panvini, *Urbs Romae*, Middleton, Vol. II. p. 357.
[2] Bergier, Vol. I. p. 8.

the conqueror of Corinth. It led straight to the Forum Boarium and the Circus Maximus[1]. Next in age comes the Mulvian (Milvian) Bridge built in 109 B.C. by the censor M. Aemilius Scaurus, who played so ignoble a part in the Jugurthan War. On it the Via Flaminia crossed the Tiber. From the left bank to the Insula Tiberina still runs the Pons Fabricius, built in 62 B.C. by L. Fabricius, a *curator viarum*[2]. It is built of two semicircular arches of peperino and tufa faced on both sides with massive blocks of travertine. From the Insula to the Janiculan bank rose the single arch of the Pons Cestius built by L. Cestius (*praefectus urbi*) in 46 B.C. Of less importance are the Pons Neronianus, begun by Gaius and finished by Nero; the Pons Agrippae, discovered in 1887 near the Ponte Sisto; and the Pons Aurelius, probably on the site of the Ponte Sisto. The date of the last-named is not known, but as it was restored in the time of Hadrian it must have been used in the first century A.D.[3]

Of the bridges in the provinces only a few can be mentioned: important commercially was the bridge of boats at Zeugma, the great crossing of the Euphrates[4]. The most famous was Trajan's bridge over the Danube at the Iron Gate, probably below Orsova. According to Dio Cassius it was made of

[1] Ov. *Fast.* VI. 477.
[2] Repeated both sides on one of the arches is this inscription: L. Fabricius C. F. Cur. viar. faciundum coeravit eidemq. probavit.
[3] The section on Roman bridges is taken from Middleton, *Remains of Ancient Rome*, Vol. II. ch. xii.
[4] Tac. *Ann.* XII. 12.

square stones and contained twenty arches, each
60 feet in breadth, 120 feet above the foundation,
and 170 feet apart. Merivale, however, concludes
from the representation on Trajan's Column that
only the piers were of masonry, the superstructure
of wood, and refuses to accept Dio's measurements[1].
However that may be, there is no doubt that the
bridge was a triumph of engineering skill, for it was
thrown over the narrowest part of the river where
the current was strongest. The architect was
Apollodorus of Damascus, who left a description of
his masterpiece. The arches were broken down by
Hadrian for fear lest the barbarians should cross
over into Roman territory, but Dio Cassius saw the
piers still standing. To this bridge Pliny doubtless
refers in the letter[2] to his friend Caninius who was
planning a poem on Trajan's Dacian wars. "You
will sing," he writes, "of fresh rivers taught to
penetrate the soil, of fresh bridges thrown over
rivers, of mountain steeps occupied by camps, of a
king who, though palace and life were lost, rose
superior to despair." Besides the Danube, the
Rhine, Euphrates and Tigris were also bridged by
Trajan. The best idea of a Roman bridge may
perhaps be gathered from the description of the
Pont du Gard near Nismes (Nemausus), erected
probably under Antoninus. It is about 880 ft. long
and 160 ft. high and is composed of three tiers of
arches, each less wide than the one below. The
whole is constructed of large stones, and no cement
has been used except for the canal on the top.

---

[1] Meriv. VIII. p. 37 *et seq.*   [2] Plin. *Epp.* VIII. 4, § 2.

More than two thousand miles away from Nismes
is a bridge which must bring home even more
forcibly the enduring nature of Roman work.   In
a desolate region[1] near Samsat, the ancient Samosata, whose only inhabitants now are a few Kurdish
herdsmen, is a Roman bridge consisting of a single
arch 112 feet in span, the keystone being 56 feet
above mean water-level.   It formed part of a frontier
road following the Euphrates line, and was restored
by Septimius Severus so perfectly that it has lasted
till to-day.

Vehicles.   With regard to the vehicles used in travelling
much information exists.   There was an ample
choice ranging from the luxurious litter (*lectica*)
borne by eight sturdy slaves to the humble *reda* or
family coach and still humbler waggon or *plaustrum*.
Beginning with the *litter* we find that it was carried
by means of poles[2] running probably through rings
fixed at the sides or perhaps attached by cords or
thongs.   The poles were often useful for thrusting
the crowd[3] out of the way and as weapons.   When
Gaius was murdered, at the first sound of the scuffle
his litter-bearers with their poles ran up to help[4].
Nothing was left undone to make the reclining
traveller comfortable.   Pliny the younger says that
when he was suffering from weak eyes[5] he was
as well sheltered in a litter as in a chamber.

---

[1] Kiakhta is the modern name of the nearest village. Hogarth,
Wandering Scholar, p. 116.

[2] asseres.

[3] Juv. VII. 132, perque forum iuvenes longo premit assere
Maedos.

[4] Suet. *Cal.* 58.   [5] Plin. *Epp.* VII. 21.

A leather head and curtains kept off the heat[1], but not always the intrusive *basiator*, from whose inconvenient affection, says Martial, there is no escape. In later times greater seclusion was obtained by the use of 'lapis specularis' or glass. Tiberius was hard-hearted enough, after his daughter-in-law and nephews had been condemned, never to let them travel except in litters with curtains sewed up all round[2]. Many luxurious fops lolled on pillows which seemed to Juvenal fit for king Sardanapalus, and drew from Seneca the indignant protest that the youths of his day were put to shame by the equestrian statue of the maiden Cloelia[3]. The litter-bearers were usually Syrian or Cappadocian slaves, six or eight in number[4], dressed in bright red travelling cloaks made often of fine wool from Canusium; hence their name of canusinati[5]. Litters might be hired at Castra Lecticariorum in the 14th region of Rome (*trans Tiberim*). The bearers formed guilds, as is seen from an inscription found in Wallachia; Cornelius Cornelianus *defensor lecticariorum* and his wife Bessa record a dedication to the goddess Nemesis[6]. As a rule litters were only used by women or by rich and luxurious men. Martial ridicules a youth, who was poorer than Irus and younger than Parthenopaeus, and yet was carried by six Cappadocian slaves[7]. Julius Caesar

---

[1] Mart. VII. 95, XI. 98, XII. 26.   [2] Suet. *Tib.* 64.

[3] Sen. *ad Marc.* 16, § 1.

[4] hexaphoron (Mart. II. 81). octaphoron (Suet. *Cal.* 43).

[5] Mart. IX. 22.   [6] *C. I. L.* Vol. III. pt 1, No. 1438.

[7] Mart. VI. 77, II. 81.

restricted their use to certain persons and times, but this was only a temporary regulation[1].

The sedan-chair or *sella* was likewise much used; in this the traveller sat, hence it was not nearly so comfortable as a litter. Augustus when consul used to go about in a chair, as did also the elder Pliny, dictating all the while to his secretary to save time[2]. Like the *lectica* the *sella gestatoria* could be closed with curtains, thus making possible the trick which Juvenal's client whose wife is away at home plays on his patron[3].

Vehicles proper may be classified as two-wheeled and four-wheeled. The most often mentioned of the former kind is the *essedum*, properly a two-wheeled chariot used by the Gauls and Britons. It was used especially on state occasions; thus Gaius was accompanied in his journey over the bridge of boats at Baiae by a suite of friends 'in essedis[4]'; in a chariot he crossed the Rhine between his troops, and in a chariot he rode, as the story tells, while certain grave and reverend senators, in their hot togas, had to race by the side. These vehicles were often profusely decorated; one of Claudius' noteworthy acts as censor was to order the purchase and destruction in his own presence of a magnificent silver chariot exposed for sale in the image market[5]. 'Silver' here probably means ornamented in Etruscan fashion with embossed metal plates[6]. Pliny the elder too speaks of the extravagance with which the

[1] Suet. *Jul.* 43.   [2] Plin. *Epp.* iii. 5, § 15, 16.
[3] Juv. i. 124.   [4] Suet. *Cal.* 19, 26, 51.
[5] Suet. *Claud.* 16.   [6] Becker, *Gallus*, p. 348 etc.

precious metals were used[1] for the decoration of all
sorts of vehicles.

The *carpentum* was a covered two-wheeled
carriage used especially by women on state occasions, as for instance by Messalina[2] and Agrippina[3]
in pursuance of a decree of the senate[4]. "Coins of
the elder Agrippina, of Livia, of the Domitillae,
wife and daughter of Vespasian, have the carpentum" (Mayor[5]). It was also used for travelling, as
by Cynthia the mistress of Propertius, who drove to
Lanuvium in a carpentum with silk curtains[6].

A vehicle especially praised by Martial is the
covinus, a sort of travelling chariot or tilbury which
could be driven by the traveller himself. He had
received a present of one from his friend Aelianus
and writes an epigram praising its 'pleasant solitude,'
for "the driver is nowhere, and the nags will hold
their tongues[7]." Of much the same kind was the
cisium or cabriolet in which Cicero's enemy Antonius
travelled at full speed from Saxa Rubra to the city[8];
but few references to it occur.

Of larger four-wheeled vehicles the most used
was the *reda* or coach, drawn by two or four horses
and constructed to carry both passengers and goods.
At first it was a family coach; thus Juvenal's
Umbricius, who was driven away by the worries of

[1] Plin. *H. N.* xxxiv. 17.   [2] Suet. *Claud.* 17.

[3] Tac. *Ann.* xii. 42.

[4] Carpenta often carried the effigies of the dead in processions.
Suet. *Claud.* 11; *Cal.* 15.

[5] Juv. ii. p. 33.   [6] Prop. iv. 8, 53.

[7] Mart. *Ep.* xii. 24.   [8] Cic. *Phil.* ii. 31. 77.

Rome, packed his whole household into a single reda[1]; later it served as a stage-coach. It was a cumbrous thing, as appears from the passage in which Juvenal says that at Rome the noise of passing coaches (*redae*) in the narrow streets, together with the din[2] when a herd of cattle was blocked, would awaken " even the Emperor Claudius or sea-calves." Lavish decorations were often seen on the body and even on the wheels; state coaches had gilded wheels, rich silver mountings and purple hangings. A leather hood was provided to keep off sun and rain.

While the master travelled in his coach, the servants usually were accommodated in the less fashionable *petorritum* or waggon. The necessity of taking a train of these on a journey is reckoned by Horace as one of the drawbacks of wealth and position[3]. Of the same class was the *carruca*, which appears from a reference in the *Digest* to have been fitted up sometimes as a sleeping-car[4] (*carruca dormitoria*). Occasionally it was gorgeously ornamented, as for instance the one which Martial says cost as much as a farm[5]. Then there was the *pilentum*, a car used for state occasions like the carpentum, but on four wheels; the *basterna*, something between a carriage and a litter, being carried by two mules in shafts one before and one behind,

[1] Juv. III. 10.   [2] Juv. III. 236—8.

[3] Hor. *Sat.* I. 6, 104.

[4] Scaev. *Dig.* XXXIV. 2. 13, quoted by Becker in Excursus in *Gallus* on vehicles.

[5] Mart. III. 72.

and lastly the rough *plaustra* and *serraca*, waggons
for heavy goods; and *axes* or drays for marble and
stone.

These wheeled vehicles were drawn by horses or
mules which were changed at stages on the journey.
A small breed of Gallic nags (*manni* or *mannuli*)
was much esteemed for speed and endurance[1].
Drivers and porters seem to have been under some
kind of supervision; we find a *superiumentarius, i.e.*
'an ex-superintendent of drivers' filling the office of
pedagogue to the young Claudius[2], and the porters
(*geruli*) were mulcted by Gaius of one-eighth of their
day's earnings.

Carriage-traffic seems to have been so general
for people of any means that but few references
occur to riding. Domitian[3], according to Suetonius,
disliking exertion, did not walk much in the city,
seldom rode when on campaigns and was constantly
carried in a litter. A century earlier, however,
Horace congratulated himself on being able to ride
on a mule to Tarentum with nothing but a saddle-
bag; the praetor Tillius had to take five slaves to
carry his cooking utensils and wine basket[4]. Persons who had not even Horace's modest competence
travelled on foot, with companions whenever possible.
Dio Chrysostom in the account of his wanderings
lays stress on the fact that during his exile he was

[1] Cf. Mart. XII. 24. Suet. *Jul.* 31; *Aug.* 36; *Cal.* 39.
Juv. III. 317.
[2] Suet. *Cl.* 2.
[3] Suet. *Dom.* § 19.
[4] Hor. *Sat.* I. 6. 107.

not only without hearth and home but without a
single attendant[1]. The poor had at least this advantage, that highwaymen left them alone. In the
Euboean Idyll[2] Dio says that he was not afraid of
following the two huntsmen because he had "only a
wretched himation." Few lines of Juvenal[3] have
become as proverbial as

"Cantabit vacuus coram latrone viator."

The luxury of the age showed itself clearly in
the elaborate preparations made for travelling. In
the preceding century Lucullus had been censured
by old-fashioned persons for taking mosaic pave-
ments and magnificent furniture on his Asiatic
campaigns; Julius Caesar[4] had done the same; but
the extravagance of the early Empire exceeds
anything we read of under the Republic. Gaius
on his journey to Germany sometimes went so fast
that the praetorian cohorts were compelled to have
their standards put on baggage-animals, and follow
in most unmilitary haste. Sometimes again he had
a fancy for travelling slowly in a palanquin and
making the common people of the cities he passed
sweep the roads for him and sprinkle them to lay
the dust[5]. He left an imitator in Nero who, we
are told, never made a journey with fewer than a
hundred travelling chariots; the mules were silver-
shod, the muleteers dressed in bright red travelling
cloaks, while the crowd of Cappadocian slaves wore

---

[1] *Or.* XL. 159 R, II. I. 59 R, XIII. 421 R.
[2] D. Chrys. *Or.* VII. 223 R.   [3] Juv. x. 19—21.
[4] Suet. *Jul.* 46.   [5] Suet. *Cal.* 43.

bracelets on their arms and ornaments on their heads and breasts[1]. Vitellius floated down the rivers of Gaul, to win and lose the Empire, on flower-decked barges carrying a quantity of dainties that disgusted even the Romans[2]. The number of slaves taken on journeys was enormous: in the cities harbingers or *anteambulones* went in front of the litters to clear the way with the words "Give place to my lord." If words did not suffice, elbows and hands were brought into play: among the minor miseries of Roman life Juvenal[3] mentions the risk of being poked with the elbow or with a hard pole in a dense crowd. Martial wittily suggests to his patron that a freedman who can keep off the crowd with a shove will be a far more serviceable visitor than an 'honestus cliens.' Outside the city walls swift Numidian riders and runners were much in vogue: we hear too of scouts to find out the condition of the road. Once on a march Tiberius' litter was stopped by the way being overgrown with brush-wood; the scout by his orders was put on the ground and scourged almost to death[4]. Augustus in spite of his simple habits liked to be attended on his journeys by his grandsons[5], who drove in front or rode at the side of his carriage.

Moralists like Seneca were indignant at such unnecessary pomp and wished "that Cato the censor could see some of the rich coxcombs with their Numidian runners stirring up a cloud of dust[6]." *Letter-carriers.*

---

[1] Suet. *Ner.* 30.
[2] Suet. *Vitell.* 16.
[3] Juv. III. 245.
[4] Suet. *Tib.* 60.
[5] Suet. *Aug.* 64.
[6] Sen. *Ep.* 87, § 9.

Yet these served for use as well as for show, in carrying letters. Official despatches, as already stated, were sent by the imperial post, but in the first century A.D. private letters were still sent by messengers (*tabellarii* or *cursores*)[1]. Letter-writing was very frequent, as the ten books of Pliny's correspondence show. A ready writer himself, he expected his friends to follow suit; in a letter to his wife Calpurnia, who was recovering in the country from an illness, he makes the rather unreasonable request that she will calm his fears by writing once and even twice a day. Again and again he asks his friends to let him hear oftener of their welfare[2]. Letters naturally did not arrive with great speed or regularity: "Your letters," writes Pliny to Romanus, "have at length reached me, and I received three at once[3]." On the borders of the Empire, *e.g.* at Tomi, the time occupied between sending the letter and receiving an answer might be as long as a year; at least Ovid makes this complaint when he sends to Gallio a letter of condolence on his wife's death[4]. Runners were also employed to convey despatches of the emperor's in or near Rome. Among the kindly acts of Titus it is recorded that he sent his own messengers to tell the mother of a conspirator that his life was safe[5]. With very different feelings, according to

[1] Plin. *Ep.* VII. 12 § 6.   Mart. III. 100. 1.
[2] *e.g.* Plin. VIII. 17.   [3] Plin. IX. 28.
[4] Ov. *Ep. ex Pont.* IV. 12,
    " Dum tua pervenit, dum littera nostra recurrens
       Tot maria ac terras permeat, annus abit."
[5] Suet. *Tit.* 9.

Tacitus, did Domitian receive by relays of runners between Alba and Rome the news of Agricola's death[1].

An explanation of the number of running foot- *Street traffic.* men, litters and sedan-chairs employed lies partly in the fact that driving in Rome and the Italian cities was forbidden except at night. The streets of Rome before the rebuilding under Nero were inconveniently narrow even for litters[2]. Augustus, we are told, when suffering from sleeplessness at night, would take a nap in his litter if it had to be put down because of a block. The tabula Heracleensis forbids carts or carriages to pass through Rome during the first ten hours of the day, the only exception being vehicles employed in public work, and those conveying the Vestal Virgins, the rex sacrorum, flamens at public sacrifices, and generals celebrating a triumph. The same grace applied to processions at public games, especially the Circensian, and to market and farm carts which had entered the town by night[3].

This heavy night traffic was an annoyance almost unendurable to sleepers in poor and crowded quarters of the city. "It costs a fortune," says Juvenal, "to be able to sleep in Rome[4]." There seems reason to doubt whether, in spite of prohibitions, vehicles did not sometimes drive within the walls by day. Seneca at one time had a town house near the Meta Sudans, the fountain close to which the Colosseum was afterwards built; he reckons the passing chariots as no

[1] Tac. *Agr*. 43.   [2] Tac. *Ann*. xv. 38.
[3] Mayor, *Juv*. II. p. 77.   [4] Juv. III. 235.

less a nuisance than his neighbours the blacksmith
and the sawyer[1]. That the practice of driving was
not frequent is however shown by the few remains
of stables and coach-houses found at Pompeii,
and also by the curious stones placed across the
road evidently for the benefit of foot-passengers
in wet weather. To these Horace probably refers
when he speaks of the 'pondera' which the would-
be magistrate must cross to greet influential voters[2].
Such blocks would present insuperable obstacles to
wheeled traffic, but not to riders or pedestrians.

The start on a long journey was usually made
from one of the city gates, where the chariot or
coach would be in readiness. So Umbricius in
Juvenal's third Satire lets the coach wait by the
Porta Capena while he bids his friend farewell[3].
While actually on the journey travellers would
read[4], write or sleep according to taste. The
Emperor Claudius, indeed, had his chariot so constructed that he could play dice in it comfortably;
this habit doubtless furnished the point to Seneca's
jest that his fit doom was to play with a bottomless
dice-box to all eternity[5]. Variety was afforded by
change of horses or mules and by stopping for the
night at inns or with friends. Very rich people
Inns. rarely used inns; they would find plenty of friends
along their route, or might even take tents and
furniture and provisions for camping out of doors.
Inns were frequented mainly, though not entirely,

[1] Sen. *Ep.* 56.
[2] Hor. *Ep.* I. 6, 1. 51.   [3] Juv. III. 1—11.
[4] Mart. XIV. 188.   Juv. III. 241.   [5] Seneca, *Apocolocyntosis.*

by the lower classes. Maecenas and Horace on the
journey to Brundisium[1] found inns at Aricia and
Appii Forum and near the shrine of Feronia: they
seem to have been uncomfortable, and at one the
water was so bad that Horace went supperless to
bed. At Formiae the travellers slept at a house
belonging to Murena, Maecenas' brother-in-law, next
day at a villula, the seventh at Cocceius' villa beyond
Caudium and on the eighth near Trivicum. Cynthia
when travelling with Propertius to Lanuvium stopped
at a taberna, while the scenes of Petronius' narrative
are mostly laid in inns. Often the building of an
inn was the beginning of a hamlet, as in the case of
the Tres Tabernae on the Appian Way[2]. Owners of
estates found it profitable to build a tavern on the
road hard by, make a freedman the host, and sell off
their wine and farm produce[3]. Sometimes inns were
built by municipal authorities; at the source of the
Clitumnus the Hispellates furnished in Pliny's time
a public bath and entertained all strangers at their
own expense[4]. Sometimes again the cost of erection
was borne by the fiscus in thinly populated or un-
civilized districts, *e.g.* in Thrace, as mentioned above[5].
In the East the inns must often have been like the
khans and caravanserais of the present day, where
travellers often furnish themselves with food, and
merely get lodging. When food was provided by
the host, it does not seem to have been dear.

---

[1] Hor. *Sat.* i. 5, ll. 2, 8, 25.   [2] Acts xxviii. 15.

[3] Vitruv. vi. 8. Varro, *R. R.* i. 2. 23, quoted by Becker, *Gallus.*
Suet. *Cl.* 38.

[4] Plin. *Epp.* viii. 8.   [5] p. 40.

Friedländer describes a relief from Aesernia in
Samnium, dating from imperial times, on which is
depicted a man in travelling dress leading a donkey
and reckoning with his hostess; the bill is given
above. Wine, like cider in Normandy, was supplied
gratis; bread was 1 as, relishes 2 asses, attendance
8 asses, and hay 2 asses, the total being 13 asses or
about 4*d.* of our money. Inns were provided on all
roads where there was much traffic; when their
resources were exhausted, officials and soldiers were
billeted on the inhabitants, a burden from which
philosophers, grammarians, rhetoricians and doctors
were relieved by Vespasian and Hadrian. At health
and pleasure resorts they were doubtless fairly comfortable. Strabo speaks of inns at Canopus[1] which
were noted for their luxury, of inns at Mount Etna
for the use of tourists who came to see the volcano,
and at Carura on the Phrygio-Carian border for
visitors to the hot springs. Inn life furnished many
illustrations to the moralists of the period. Epictetus[2]
compares those who do not pass on quickly from
rhetoric to philosophy to loiterers at an inn. "Men,"
he declares, "generally act as a traveller would do
on his way to his own country when he enters a
pleasant inn and being pleased with it remains there.
'Man, you have forgotten your purpose; you were
not travelling to this inn, but you were passing
through it.' 'But this is a pleasant inn.' 'And
how many inns are pleasant?' And how many
meadows are pleasant? yet only for passing through.'"

[1] Strab. p. 801, 578.   [2] Epict. *Diss.* II. 18. 2.

One of the great drawbacks to travelling by road in the South and East was the heat. Pliny the younger, writing to Septicius, says that he has had a good journey to the country, but that some of his servants had been made ill by the excessive heat: his reader Encolpius[1] had been injured internally through the dust settling on his lungs. Wherever possible journeys in hot weather were made by night[2]: when there was no moon torches were carried, which no doubt often diversified the monotony of the journey by going out. This happened to Julius Caesar on the night before he crossed the Rubicon: in the darkness he lost his way and did not recover it for some hours.

With regard to the speed of travelling we are told that Mallius Glaucia who brought to Ameria the news of Sextus Roscius' death travelled 56 miles in 10 hours of the night: the vehicle he used was the light two-wheeled *cisium* or cabriolet[3]. Such a speed was of course extraordinary. The Dictator Julius was famed for his rapid journeys; in a hired coach he travelled 100 miles a day[4]. The highest speed recorded is that of Tiberius, who hastened from Ticinum through Rhaetia to Germany, reaching his brother Drusus just in time to be with him before he died[5]. He covered a distance of 200 miles in 24 hours: ordinary travellers would take at least

Rate of travelling.

---

[1] Plin. *Epp.* VIII. 1, 2.
[2] See Suet. *Aug.* 29, 53 and *Iul.* 31.   Juv. x. 19—21.   Suet. *Tib.* 6.   Tac. *Hist.* III. 79.
[3] Cic. *pro Rosc. Amer.* 7. 19.   [4] Suet. *Iul.* 57.
[5] Val. Max. 5. 3.

four days. Another very quick journey was that of
the freedman Icelus, who brought the news of Nero's
death to Galba in Spain within seven days, a time
which seemed incredibly short[1]. The speed of the
imperial post averaged five miles an hour: the
distance between Antioch and Byzantium (747 miles)
was accomplished in a little under six days: hired
vehicles would take longer. From Ostia to Tarraco
(163 miles) usually took five days, but Pliny the
elder once took only four[2]. From Naples to Toledo
took six days with post-horses; from Brundisium to
Rome was a ten days' leisurely journey[3] according
to Ovid:

> "Luce minus decima dominam venietis in urbem
>   Ut festinatum non faciatis iter."

Maecenas and Horace however took fifteen days[4].
It seems that travellers in carriages as a rule[5]
covered from forty to fifty miles a day or a little
over: if they wished for speed, they had, as Seneca[6]
says, to cut down their baggage and dismiss their
attendants. A foot-passenger in good training might

---

[1] Plut. *Galb.* 7.   [2] Plin. *H. N.* xix. 4.
[3] Ov. *Epp. ex Pont.* iv. 5. 3.   [4] Hor. *Sat.* i. 5.
[5] The ordinary rate of 40 miles a day for carriages is given by
Martial, who tells his friend Flavus that Bilbilis is reached from
Tarraco (200 miles away) in five days (x. 104).

> Hispanae pete Tarraconis arces;
> Illinc te rota tollet, et citatus
> Altam Bilbilin et tuum Salonem
> Quinto forsan essedo videbis.

(*i.e.* in the fifth stage and so on the fifth day).
[6] Sen. *Cons. ad Helv.* c. 12.

expect to walk from twenty-six to twenty-seven
Roman miles in the day.

A question of some interest with regard to first *Security*
century travel is that of security. The evidence is *of travel.*
rather contradictory; some writers extol the safety
conferred by the imperial rule, while others lament
over the effrontery of highwaymen near Rome itself.
On the whole it is clear that brigandage had been
rife during the last century of the Republic but was
vigorously suppressed by the emperors except in
mountainous or outlying districts. The punishment for robbers was crucifixion. In Strabo's time
the Pamphylians and the dwellers on the Mysian
Olympus[1] were much given to brigandage, and the
Corsicans[2] gained their living by the same means.
The preventive measures taken in Asia Minor by
Augustus will be dealt with in a later section; those
for Italy are described in some detail by Suetonius
in a passage which clearly shows their necessity.
"Several disorders most pernicious to the state
had either continued through habit and the licence
of civil war or had even arisen through peace:
numbers of highwaymen openly showed themselves
armed with swords as if for self-defence; travellers
all over the country were carried off without
distinction between freeman and slave, and kept
in barracoons (*ergastula*): many associations were
formed, under the guise of new clubs, for the
committal of every kind of villainy[3]. The emperor
checked brigandage by setting military posts in

[1] Strab. pp. 570, 574.   [2] Strab. p. 224.
[3] Suet. *Aug.* 32.

suitable spots, ordered an inspection of the barracoons and dissolved the associations except those of
ancient date and lawful character." Tiberius was
equally vigorous in searching for those who had
been kidnapped and increasing the number of military posts throughout Italy. Sardinia in particular
was infested by brigands ; to suppress them he sent
four thousand freedmen, chiefly Jews, with the cynical
remark that if they were killed by the detestable
climate it would be small loss[1]. Inscriptions in the
Jura region show that a prefect existed in the first
century especially for suppressing robbers : similarly
we learn that an official under Drusus Caesar extir-
pated the robber-bands on the Hellespont[2].

The success of such efforts was, of course, only
partial; " so long," says Dio Cassius[3], " as human
nature remains unchanged, brigandage will continue."
In the time of Augustus we are told that the praetor
Quintus Gallus was ostensibly banished from Rome
on the charge of conspiracy, but really murdered
in secret in the hope that his disappearance might
be put down to death by shipwreck or robbers[4].
The execution of two brigands was commanded
by Nero on the occasion of his uttering his famous
wish that he had never learned to write[5]. Umbricius

[1] Tac. _Ann._ ii. 85.

[2] _C. I. G._ 3612, ἡ βουλὴ καὶ ὁ δῆμος ἐτείμησαν Τίτον Οὐ(α)λέριον
Πρόκλον τὸν φροντιστὴν Δρούσου Καίσαρος, καθελόντα τὰ ἐν Ἑλλησ-
πόντῳ λῃστήρια καὶ ἐν ἅπασιν ἀνεπιβάρητον φυλάξαντα τὴν πόλιν.
(Fragment of a column found near Halileli in the rubbish of a
temple, probably to the Thymbraean Apollo.)

[3] Dio Cass. xxxvi.   [4] Suet. _Aug._ 27.
[5] Sen. _de Clem._ ii. 1.

in his long catalogue of Roman plagues mentions
the highwayman who often sets to work with the
sword while the rest of the gang lie concealed in the
Pontine marshes or the wood near Cumae[1]. Pliny
the younger is informed by a friend that Robustus,
an 'eques splendidus,' has not been heard of since
he reached Ocriculum ; he fears that the fate of the
missing man has been that of a fellow-townsman of
his own who set out for the army, but disappeared
without a trace[2]. In Palestine especially travelling
was unsafe, as is shown by Josephus and the New
Testament. Theudas, Tholomaeus, Judas the Gali-
laean and his sons Jacobus and Simon were the most
prominent of those who were driven to brigandage
in their desperate resistance to Roman rule. How
far they succeeded in interrupting communication
is seen from the account of St Paul's hurried ride
from Jerusalem to escape from the conspirators
against his life. He was accompanied to Antipatris
by no fewer than four hundred and seventy soldiers,
horsemen and spearmen, the horsemen continuing
to escort him as far as Caesarea[3].

Inscriptions give abundant evidence in the same
direction for the first and succeeding centuries. At
Mehadia[4] is recorded the murder of a magistrate of
the 'municipium Drobetarum' by brigands. Near
the same place Bassus, the quaestor of the same
township, met a like death[5]. Similarly at Salonae

[1] Juv. III. 305—8, cf. XIII. 145, x. 20.
[2] Plin. *Epp.* VI. 25.   [3] Acts xxiii. *vv.* 23, 31, 32.
[4] *C. I. L.* III. 1, 1559.
[5] *C. I. L.* III. 1, 1579.

C. Tadius, a municipal magistrate (*sevir*) was carried
of by highwaymen[1]. Most pathetic of all is the
record at Spalatum of the little Iulia Restituta,
ten years old, who was killed by robbers for the
sake of her jewels[2]. " Dis Manibus Iuliae Restitutae
infelicissimae interfectae annorum x causa orna-
mentorum Iulius Restitutus et Statia Pudentilla
parentes."

Yet the above evidence must not be pressed too
far. If communication was often insecure under the
early Empire, it had been insecure before, and has
often been so since. Mommsen's words may apply
to other things than the imperial government.
" Even now there are various regions of the East,
as of the West, as regards which the imperial period
marks a climax very modest in itself but withal
never attained before or since[3]." Syria and Palestine,
Anatolia, Turkey and Morocco are far worse off with
respect to communication than they were then.
The route which Aurelian took to Palmyra is now,
according to Merivale, too desolate to be traversed
by an army. Asia Minor is studded with the
ruins of what were once flourishing towns in close
communication with one another. Even in the
West it is only since the introduction of railways
that ancient travel has been surpassed by modern
in speed and safety[4]. In 1846, says Friedländer,

[1] *C. I. L.* 2544.

[2] *C. I. L.* 2399, cf. ibid. 158.

[3] Mommsen, *Provinces*, Vol. I. p. 5.

[4] For French roads in the 17th century see M. Hanotaux,
Richelieu, I. pp. 164 and 174.

the King of Naples and his troops, when on a
military promenade, lost their way and were not
heard of in the capital for a fortnight. In 1872
there were scarcely any good roads in Sicily and
travelling in the interior was very difficult, yet in
Roman days there were 220 miles of road connecting
all the towns of the coast, and the chief of the
interior with Panormus (Palermo). The completeness of the imperial road-system in Spain has been
referred to above. In 1830 there was only one main
route from Madrid to the other chief towns of the
peninsula; a few provincial roads were passable for
carriages, but the greater part of the country was a
perfect wilderness save for foot and bridle paths.
From Madrid to Toledo, a distance of 25 miles, there
was not a single branch road[1].

Up to the eighteenth century the state of the
roads in England was just as bad; in 1685 the main
lines were still those traced out in Roman days:
one of the things for which the nation might have
thanked William III. was his vigorous action against
the highwaymen of Hounslow Heath. The lack of
communication between town and country is vividly
described in the Annual Register for 1761[2]. "It is
scarce half a century ago since the inhabitants of
distant counties were regarded as a species almost
as different from those of the metropolis as the
natives of the Cape of Good Hope....A journey
into the country was then considered almost as
great an undertaking as a voyage to the Indies.

[1] From Friedländer.
[2] Lecky, *Hist. of the* 18th *Cent.* Vol. VII. p. 216.

The old family coach was sure to be stored with all sorts of luggage and provisions, and perhaps in the course of the journey a whole village together with their teams were called in to dig the heavy vehicles out of the clay." The 'gentlemen of the road' need only be mentioned; they disappeared with the improvement of roads and the introduction of stage-coaches. Yet even twentieth-century England might well imitate the foresight and thoroughness which were the characteristics of the imperial system of communication.

CHAPTER IV.

COMMUNICATION BY SEA.

So far, only that mode of communication has *Communi-* been described which the Romans carried out with *cation by sea.* a definite aim, viz., the road-system. Their maritime communications were far more the result of circumstances, geographical and political. Not till several centuries after the foundation of the city did Rome become a naval power. "The sea," said Arnold, "deserved to be hated by the old aristocracies," and as late as 218 B.C. Flaminius carried a law forbidding any senator or senator's son to own a vessel of greater burden than 300 amphorae[1]. Yet Rome was admirably situated to be the emporium of Latin commerce[2]; long before she had traded with Massilia, Sicily, and even Greece. The naval supremacy of Carthage, threatening her long sea-frontier and limiting her commerce, drove her, however, unwillingly, to create a war-navy. There was abundance of triremes and merchant-ships belonging to the Romans themselves and their allies; what were needed were ships of the line (quinqueremes) for which a stranded Carthaginian

---

[1] Liv. xxi. 63.   [2] Mommsen, *Hist. of Rome*, i. p. 49.

penteres served as a model. The fleet played an important part in the first Punic war, and when the struggle was resumed one of the main causes of Hannibal's defeat was the fact that the Romans held the Tuscan Sea. He was thus driven to his long and disastrous Alpine march, and cut off from his base in Spain[1].

In the 'most inglorious epoch of Roman history,' the years between the fall of Carthage and the death of Sulla, the fleet fell into utter neglect. "There was[2] hardly any longer a Roman vessel of war, and the vessels which the subject cities were required to build and maintain were not sufficient, so that Rome was not only absolutely unable to carry on a naval war, but was not even in a position to check the trade of piracy." Rome smarted for her negligence in the Mithradatic wars, when the pirate fleets were ranged on the side of her enemies. Commerce was almost at a standstill, corn was scarce in Italy and the city, temples and islands were ransacked; "the provinces equipped squadrons and raised coastguards, or at any rate were taxed for the purpose, and yet pirates appeared to plunder the provincials with as much regularity as the Roman governors[3]." So insupportable was the evil that at length the duty of suppressing it was confided to Pompeius by the Gabinian Law of 67 B.C. The result was that, within forty-nine days after his

[1] Mahan, in *The Influence of the Sea Power upon History*, *ad init.*

[2] Mommsen, *Hist. of Rome*, III. p. 405.

[3] Ibid. IV. p. 76.

appearance in the Levant, the great pirate-haunt, Cilicia, was subdued. Few circumstances show the incapacity of the government at that time more clearly than the way in which the performance of such an elementary duty was celebrated as a glorious victory. After this, piracy did not for centuries appear in the Mediterranean as an organized system.

The importance of maritime command was realized by Augustus in his contest with Sextus Pompeius, who for some time was master of the sea, and stopped the Roman corn-supplies. The victories of Naulochus over Sextus, and Actium over Antony and Cleopatra, among other great issues, decided that Italy should enjoy a maritime supremacy; from them date the completeness of communication which for centuries turned the Mediterranean into an 'Italian lake.'

The ships afloat in the first century A.D. were of *War-ships.* various kinds. The imperial fleet was permanently stationed off Italy in two squadrons at Ravenna and Misenum; it consisted mainly of triremes and the light Liburnian[1] biremes which had done good service at Actium. The construction of rowing

[1] These are frequently mentioned throughout the first and following centuries; in time Liburna came to mean a man-of-war. See the following passages:—

Tac. *Hist.* v. 23. In the sea-fight between Civilis and Cerealis the former had biremes and boats with tackling like Liburnian vessels.

Tac. *Hist.* III. 47. Mucianus collected at Byzantium "lectissimas Liburnicarum."

Suet. *Nero*, 34. Agrippina came from Bauli to Baiae in a "liburnica."

vessels had not altered much in principle since the
days of the Athenian navy though much larger
ships had been built, such as the sixteen-ranked
ship of Demetrius Poliorcetes and the forty-ranked
of Ptolemy Philopator, which latter could only
venture to sea in smooth water[1]. The trireme was
manned, it has been calculated, by 175 men; penteres by 310. The length of a trireme judging from
the remains of the docks at Zea was 149 ft. and the
breadth 14 feet; the tonnage 232. The arrangement
of oars in three tiers was doubtless the same as in
Athenian days. War-ships were not meant to keep
the sea for long and therefore had hardly anything
to carry besides their crew. Even one with ten
banks of oars could not carry more than three
thousand talents[2].

The timber used for war-ships was fir, which
was carefully seasoned; the seams were caulked
with tow, etc., and fixed with wax or tar. The
same materials, mixed with paint, protected the
outer planking. Often the hulls were painted with
designs; the pirates had theirs coloured to match
the waves. As regards masts and sails, there seem
to have been a mainmast with a yard that carried
a square sail below, and a triangular sail above.
Besides the mainmast there were sometimes two

[1] Guhl and Koner, p. 261.
[2] In the time of Dionysius of Halicarnassus (30—8 B.C.) the
Tiber was navigable up to Rome for ten-banked war-ships; we
know also that any merchant-ship carrying more than 3000
talents had to anchor at Ostia and discharge part of her cargo.
Hence 3000 talents was the limit for the weight on board a
war-ship. (Torr, *Ancient Ships*.)

smaller masts, a foremast or bowsprit with a yard
and square sail only, and also a mizen with perhaps
a similar yard and sail. War-ships, however, used
the oar rather than sails, so as to be independent
of the wind. Hence as a recent naval writer has
pointed out, the ancient galley had some features
in common with the modern man-of-war[1].

For merchant-vessels speed was not so essential *Merchant-*
as cheapness of transit; hence they carried large *men.*
sails and only a few oars (about twenty) to bring the
ship's head round, and for use in emergencies. A
merchantman trying to make some headway with
her oars only is compared by Aristotle to an insect
feebly buzzing along on wings too small for its body,
after the manner of cockchafers and bees; whereas
the war-ship under way, rhythmically dipping her
vast mass of oars, was commonly compared to a bird
on its flight[2]. The bulky proportions of a merchant
vessel compared with the slenderness of a war-galley
accounted for the epithet given to it of στρόγγυλος.
The ratio of its length to its breadth was usually
3 or 4 to 1, whereas in the case of war-ships it was 15
to 2. The sails were large, especially on Alexandrian
vessels: up to the time of Augustus they were made
of hemp often coloured and painted with devices[3];
later Egyptian linen was used as being lighter[4].
The keels were of pine, but all large merchantmen

---

[1] Mahan, *Influence of Sea Power upon History, ad init.*
[2] Arist. *de animalium incessu*, quoted by Torr.
[3] The edges were bound with strips of hide, especially of hyena
and seal, which were thought to keep off lightning.
[4] Plin. *H. N.* XIX. 1.   Meriv. IV. p. 390.

S.   6

had false keels of oak for protection when they were
hauled ashore or dragged overland[1]. Fir or pine was
used for the mast and oars, papyrus, flax or hemp,
occasionally hide, for the ropes.

Some sort of flag seems to have been used for
signalling, and to distinguish the admiral's ship in
the case of war-vessels[2]. Large and slow merchant
ships had a corbes or basket on the top of the mast
and were hence called 'corbitae[3].' As in Aristo-
phanes' days the ship's 'eyes' were painted on her
bows[4]. War-ships showed a helmet, swift cruisers
the petasus, and ships on a mission of truce the
caduceus. Ships seem to have had names as in
modern times, e.g. the ship in which Ovid sailed to
Tempyra from the Corinthian Gulf was named the
'Minerva'; the Alexandrian vessel in which St Paul
performed part of his journey to Rome had for a
sign 'Castor and Pollux.' Among other appurte-
nances of an ancient ship may be mentioned the
sounding lead which was greased in use to bring
up samples of the sea-bottom[5], the gangway for
getting on board and the poles for pushing off from
shore, also the 'fenders[6]' (ἀσκώματα) for preventing

[1] Suetonius says that Gaius ordered the triremes on which he
had sailed the Northern Ocean to be conveyed to Rome by land
for the most part.   Suet. Cal. 47.

[2] Cf. Tac. Hist. v. 22, "navis praetoria vexillo insignis."

[3] Cf. Plaut. Poen. 3. 1. 4, "homines spissigradissimos, tardiores
quam corbitae sunt in tranquillo mari.

[4] Arist. Ach. 97. Aesch. Supp. 716.   [5] Acts xxvii. 28.

[6] Arist. Ach. 97. For representations of ancient ships, see
Torr's Ancient Ships, and Baumeister, Art. Seewesen, especially
pp. 1624 and 1634.

the ship's side from getting rubbed against the landing place. A merchant ship of any size had a boat, sometimes two or three, towed astern. This was meant for the safety of the crew in case of shipwreck or for communication with the shore; the boat could be hoisted up in stormy weather as was done on St Paul's voyage:—" And running under the lee of a small island called Clauda we were able with difficulty to secure the boat[1]." Another reference is found in a letter of Pliny's describing Lake Vadimon, on which were floating islands. " You may frequently see one of the larger islands sailing along with the lesser joined to it like a ship with its longboat[2]."

The average tonnage of a merchant ship is a difficult point to determine. Pliny speaks of vessels carrying 3000 amphorae ; the highest figure mentioned is 10,000 talents or 250 tons. Huge vessels were built especially in Alexandria for the transport of obelisks or of marble in the rough. The ' Acatus,' the first Alexandrian ship that entered the roadstead at Ostia during Augustus' principate, brought an obelisk which was erected by Gaius in the Circus Maximus. It carried 1200 passengers besides a cargo of papyrus, nitrum, pepper, linen and spices[3]. Another enormous vessel under Gaius brought the obelisk for the Vatican Circus and four blocks of stone for the base : the mast was so huge that it could only be clasped by four men. Claudius used the hull to form part of the foundation for his new

[1] Acts xxvii. 16 R.V.
[2] Plin. *Epp.* viii. 20; cf. Philostrat. *Vit. Apoll.* iv. 9.
[3] Plin. *H. N.* xvi. 201, and xxxvi. 2.

harbour at Ostia: towers were built on it at Puteoli, then it was towed to the required spot and sunk.

Specially important were the large vessels used for corn transport. These usually voyaged in fleets, but we have instances of single ships making a voyage, as that in which St Paul went from Myra in Lycia to Melita. Probably it had run directly across the Levant from Alexandria, as was possible if the wind were westerly[1]. While the Etesian winds were blowing—from July 20th to the end of August—Alexandrian ships ran to the Syrian coast and thence tacked along Cilicia and Pamphylia using the land-breezes and the steady westerly current along the coast. The slowness of the process is shown by an addition in the Syriac version of the Acts, viz. that fifteen days were spent in beating along the southern coast of Asia Minor. Of course the reverse run from Lycia to the Syrian coast was an easy matter.

Lucian in his dialogue 'The Ship[2]' describes an Alexandrian vessel which had tried to run direct to Myra and had met with foul weather. On the seventh day of the voyage it was off the westernmost point of Cyprus, C. Acamas, whence it was blown to Sidon by westerly gales. On the tenth day from Sidon it was caught in a storm at the Chelidonian islands and would have been wrecked but that "the sailors' gods in pity showed a light," and the Lycian coast was recognised. Even after this escape its

---

[1] Ramsay, *St Paul the Traveller*, p. 314 *et seq*.

[2] Lucian, *Navig.* 1—6.

course was slow, and not till the seventieth day after first starting did it reach Athens.

Its arrival, says the story, caused great excitement; for by Lucian's day the port of Athens was almost deserted. Samippus seizes the opportunity to go aboard, and comes back to his friends eager to tell all the wonderful things he has seen. " What a big ship she is, a hundred and twenty cubits long, the shipwright said, and more than a quarter of this in breadth : from deck to bottom there are nine and twenty cubits. And then how huge the mast is, and what a great yard-arm and what forestays ! To see the stern curving up gently like a goose's neck, and the prow stretching out so far, with the image on both sides of Isis, after whom the ship is named ! Then the decoration, the paintings and the bright-coloured topsail, the anchors and capstans and windlasses and the cabins aft—all this seemed to me simply wonderful. Why, you might compare the number aboard to an army, and enough corn was there, I am told, to feed the whole of Attica for a year[1]."

The numbers carried on the Egyptian ships do indeed seem to have been large. Josephus[2] says that 600 were on board a ship that took prisoners from Judaea to Rome. The rhetor Aristides writing in the second century A.D. gives one thousand as the

---

[1] Cf. Epict. *Frag.* 14. "As you would not choose to sail in a *large and decorated ship* ornamented with gold, and be drowned ; so do not choose to dwell in a large and costly house and be disturbed by cares."

[2] *Vit.* 3.

maximum. Philo Judaeus extols the merits of his
fellow countrymen as mariners. " When Agrippa
was about to set out to take possession of his kingdom, Gaius advised him to avoid the voyage from
Brundisium to Syria, which was long and troublesome,
and rather to take the shorter one by Alexandria
and to wait for the periodical winds: for he said
that the vessels which set forth from that harbour
were fast sailers, and that the pilots were most
experienced men who guided their ships as skilful
drivers drive their horses, keeping them straight in
the right course[1]." Agrippa took this advice; "going
down to Dicaearchia (*i.e.* Puteoli) and seeing some
Alexandrian vessels in the harbour looking all ready
and fit to put to sea, he embarked with all his officers,
and had a good voyage, arriving after a few days at
his journey's end." In all probability the Alexandrian
corn-fleet was part of the Imperial service, as ocean-
liners are now subsidized by Government for carrying
the mails. Any delay might have serious conse-
quences for the emperor himself. Suetonius tells
us that during scarcity of bread at Rome, Claudius
was mobbed, and had to get into his palace by a
back-door. We are not surprised to hear that after
this he tried every possible expedient for keeping
up the supplies even in winter. He offered a
fixed amount of profit to the dealers, and under-
took the risk of loss by storm, besides affording
every convenience to the builders of merchant-
vessels[2].

[1] Phil. Jud. *In Flacc.* v.   [2] Suet. *Claud.* 19.

For coasting voyages smaller vessels (called *ora-riae*) were naturally used. Pliny writes to Trajan[1] that he has safely sailed past C. Malea[2] to Ephesus, and intends thence to reach his province of Bithynia partly 'orariis navibus,' partly by conveyances, since the Etesian winds prevented continuous sailing. The coasting trade must have been very considerable in the Mediterranean : it would be comparatively little liable to contrary winds, since the land breezes could be utilized. An instance is to be found in the Acts of the Apostles : St Paul coasted to Myra in a ship bound for Adramyttium in Mysia[3]. Again Plutarch in one of his most amusing essays asks the borrower of money, " Can you not be a schoolmaster or tutor, or porter, or sailor, or make coasting voyages[4] ? " In the Aegean ships are scarcely ever out of sight of land, and for many places in Greece communication by sea was far quicker than by road.

Passengers seem to have often travelled by merchant-ships, especially for long voyages. One of these conveyed Titus on his hasty journey from the East to Rhegium and Puteoli[5]. A passage in Plutarch shows that triremes were sometimes used by the very rich. " But just as people on sea, timid and prone to sea-sickness, think they will suffer less

[1] Plin. *Epp. ad Trai.* 15 (26).

[2] On account of the danger in sailing round C. Malea the phrase ὑπὲρ Μαλέαν became proverbial.

[3] Acts xxvii. 2, 5.

[4] Plutarch *Against borrowing money*. Cf. Phil. Jud. *De leg. &c.* § 33.

[5] Suet. *Tib.* 5.

on board a merchantman than on a boat, and for the
same reason shift their quarters to a trireme, but do
not attain anything by these changes, for they take
with them their timidity and qualmishness; so
changes of life do not remove the troubles and
sorrows of the soul[1]." With this may be compared Horace's 'priva triremis' and the 'aerata
triremis,' which nevertheless "is not free from
care[2]."

We read also of *vectoriae*, apparently for passengers, not for cargo. In one of these Julius Caesar
crossed the Hellespont after Pharsalia[3]. In the
second century they were more used than in the
first. From about 50 B.C. to 100 A.D. the vessel
specially constructed for passenger traffic was the
phaselus. This seems to have served the purpose of
the modern yacht; Martial[4] speaks of the "waves
lively yet quiet, carrying the painted gondola with
the aid of the breeze." It was however fit for a
long voyage in fair weather, even, according to
Catullus[5], from Pontus to Italy. The epithet 'fra-
gilis' applied to it by Horace[6] shows that it could
not stand a gale.

With regard to life on board in fair weather
there is a curious lack of information; it is the
exceptional rather than the ordinary that has come
down to us, and we hear far more of storms than of
safe voyages. The plan of St Luke's narrative

<hr>

[1] Plut. *On Contentedness of Mind* (trans. by Shilleto).
[2] Hor. *Epp.* I. 1. 93.   *Od.* III. 1. 37.   [3] Suet. *Iul.* 63.
[4] Mart. x. 30.   [5] Cat. 4.
[6] Hor. *Od.* III. 2. 28.

precluded needless digressions; Ovid might have told much about his journey to Tomi, but has omitted nearly all that could interest anyone but himself. One or two chance allusions, however, may be worth quoting. Dio Chrysostom in his third oration says: "Many in calm weather pass their time in dicing or in singing or in feasting all day long, but when the storm overtakes them, they cover their heads and wait for what is to happen. Others again settle themselves to sleep, and do not even get up till they have reached the harbour[1]." The passengers seem to have provided their own food, to judge from Epictetus, who asks, "What do you do when you leave a ship? Do you take away the helm or the oars? What then do you take away? You take what is your own, your bottle and your wallet[2]." It may perhaps be possible that in the opening of Lucian's dialogue 'The Ferryboat' he is parodying the custom of keeping a passenger list. Clotho before setting sail for Hades receives from Hermes and enters on Charon's way-bill the names, nationality and manner of death of the various passengers.

Among the greatest aids to navigation in the *Harbours.* first century A.D. was the attention paid by the best of the emperors to the improvement of harbours of refuge. A work, which to Vergil and Horace[3] was one of the noblest achievements of Roman engineering, was Agrippa's Portus Iulius. This was constructed by Octavius' orders to secure a harbour

---

[1] Dio Chrys. *Or.* III. 122 R.
[2] Epict. *Diss.* I. 24; cf. Juv. XII. 60.
[3] Verg. *Georg.* II. 160—4. Hor. *A. P.* 63—65.

on the west of Italy equal to those at Ravenna
and Brundisium. On the Campanian coast between
Misenum and Puteoli lay the lagoons of Avernus
and Lucrinus : together they made something like
the figure 8, the two loops being connected by a
neck of land a mile wide ; the southern or Lucrine
lake was sheltered from the Bay of Baiae only by a
ridge of shingle. Agrippa seems to have united the
lakes by a canal, faced the outer ridge with stone-
work and driven through it a channel to admit
ships. According to Suetonius the possession of
this harbour largely contributed to the victory of
Augustus over Sextus Pompeius[1].

In the time of the first Emperor Ostia, the port
of Rome, was " a city without a harbour," on account
of the mud brought down by the Tiber. Large
vessels were therefore forced to ride at anchor in the
open roadstead at great risk, while their cargoes were
unloaded into barges and towed up to Rome. Other
vessels were themselves towed up the Tiber after
part of their cargo had been landed[2]. The Dictator
Caesar had planned docks at Ostia, but nothing was
done till Claudius constructed that magnificent
harbour[3] which was one of the most useful of his
public works. In spite of the timidity of his engi-
neers and the enormous expense and labour involved,
a basin was dug about two miles north of Ostia,
communicating with the river by a canal. Two

---

[1] Suet. *Aug.* 16. Strab. 245.
[2] Strab. 231, 232.
[3] Suet. *Cl.* 20. Dio Cass. LX. 11. Plin. *H. N.* IX. § 14, XVI.
202. Juv. XII. 75 (with Mayor's notes).

moles, right and left, with a breakwater between them, protected the port. A lighthouse was erected on the breakwater, modelled on the Pharos of Alexandria.

Yet even this magnificent structure was inadequate for the growing needs of the city. Trajan added an inner basin or dock, hexagonal in form, surrounded with quays and extensive ranges of buildings for magazines. The same emperor, who 'built the world over,' made at Ancona a haven of which an arch still remains, and his harbour at Centumcellae furnished a theme for the rhetoric of the younger Pliny. He describes the breaking of the force of the waves by the artificial island, which was being raised with huge stones sunk from pontoons and surmounted by large piles : the undertaking, he adds, will prove of vast benefit by affording a safe refuge to ships on a long and dangerous coast[1].

The improvements at Ostia caused the decline of Puteoli, which had been the great harbour of Rome, especially for the corn-trade. Massilia and Forum Iulii in the Narbonensis possessed good harbours, and the same may be inferred for Galles from the importance of its trade and the habit of its merchants to "live for the most part at sea[2]." The harbours of Asia Minor, Ephesus especially, will be described in another section. Syria was not so fortunate, and Seleucia the port of Antioch was not fitted for much commerce in spite of the efforts of the Flavian and succeeding emperors to construct docks and piers[3].

---

[1] Plin. *Epp.* VI. 31.   Meriv. VIII. p. 52.
[2] Strab. III. 5. 3.   [3] Mommsen, *Provinces*, II. p. 128.

Most famous of all the harbours of the Empire was that of Alexandria, which is mentioned by Dio Chrysostom in his oration to the Alexandrians as one of the chief glories of their city[1]. The light on the Pharos or white marble tower, built by Sostratus of Cnidus and visible for more than seven geographical miles out to sea, served as a model for the lights at Ostia and even on the shore of the Northern Ocean[2]. That such protection to sailors was regularly provided at harbours we gather from a fragment of Epictetus which compares the services of a benefactor of a troubled state to the fire-lights in harbours, which by a few pieces of wood raise a great flame and give sufficient direction to the ships which are wandering on the sea[3].

A strong motive for carrying out harbour works lay in the fact that navigation as a rule was confined to the summer months, hence accommodation had to be found for the large number of ships necessarily employed in this brief time. The familiar instance may be quoted of the desire felt by the majority on board St Paul's vessel to reach Phoenice in Crete because it was ' more commodious to winter in ' than the Fair Havens[4]. The common practice is described by Philo in the following passage. " The news was spread abroad that Gaius was sick while the weather was still suitable for sailing; for it was the beginning of autumn, which is the last season during which

---

[1] Dio Chrys. *Or.* xxxii. 36 R.

[2] Strab. p. 792.   Suet. *Cal.* 46.   [3] Epict. *Frag.* 78.

[4] Acts xxvii. 8, 12; cf. the phrase λιμὴν παραχειμαστικός, *Geogr. Min.* 2. 459.

mariners can safely make voyages, and during which
in consequence they all return from foreign parts to
every quarter to their own native ports and harbours
of refuge, especially all who exercise a prudent care
not to be compelled to pass the winter in a foreign
country[1]." So too Gyges in Horace's Ode tried too
late to cross from Epirus to Italy on his way home from
Bithynia and had to wait at Oricus till spring should
open the sea. The custom furnished the same poet
with the fine simile of Rome watching for Augustus
even as a mother for her sailor-boy who is in Egypt
or Syria, waiting for the spring to cross the Carpa-
thian sea. The sailing season which began in spring
(February or March) ended with the setting of the
Pleiades on the 11th of November. The remainder
of the year counted as winter, but the pirates had in
the day of their power "compelled men from fear of
death to rush upon death, while now greed of gain
gave the like impulse[2]."

Some strong motive certainly was needed to
make men face the winter storms in days when
the mariner's compass was unknown. Winter voyages are therefore spoken of as exceptional and
dangerous. Only under the compulsion of religion
would Philo and his companions have sailed in mid-
winter from Alexandria to Italy to deprecate the
erection of a colossus in the Holy of Holies. The
strength of Jewish feeling is seen in his words,
"yet we found a winter of misery awaiting us on
shore far more grievous than any storm at sea[3]."

[1] Phil. Jud. *De Leg.* II.　　　[2] Plin. II. 17 *et seq.*
[3] Phil. Jud. *De Leg.* 29.

Flaccus, the enemy of the Jews who, says Philo,
"had filled all the elements with his impieties," set
sail from Alexandria at the beginning of winter, and
by a just doom suffered innumerable hardships
before reaching Italy[1]. Communication between
Rome and the provinces had to go on to some
extent during the winter, certainly for official purposes ; exiles too were then deported, as is seen by
the case of Ovid, who reckoned his misfortunes as
infinitely increased by the hardships of the winter.
In the *Tristia* he describes his voyage from Cen-
chreae to Samothrace and his fervent hope that his
ship, the ' Minerva,' which he left off Tempyra may
have a safe passage to Tomi[2]. By taking the land
route through the region of the Bistones he escaped
much of the misery of a winter voyage, yet he
laments most piteously over the waves rising mountains high, the wilderness of sea and air, and the
helpless terror even of the captain.

Storms and ship-wrecks. The voyagers of ancient times even in the
summer were often liable to storm and shipwreck.
Sudden squalls had at all times to be dreaded,
to say nothing of such local and violent winds
as the ' circius' off Gallia Narbonnensis, which
on two occasions[3] nearly wrecked the Emperor
Claudius, or the ' Caicias[4]' which, centuries before,
destroyed the Persian ships off Magnesia, or the
' sciron' which was unknown except at Athens[5].

[1] Phil. *in Flacc.* 13.   [2] Ov. *Trist.* II. 11.
[3] Suet. *Claud.* 17.
[4] Called also Hellespontias, Herod. 7. 188.
[5] Strab. xxviii. 391. Plin. *H. N.* II. 117 *et seq.* says of the
sciron that it was "reliquae Graeciae ignotus." In the same

St Luke's account of St Paul's voyage[1] to Italy
is the fullest description we have of storm and shipwreck in the Mediterranean during the first century.
We read of the slow progress against the wind past
the Lycian coast to Crete, of the tempestuous
Euraquilo which suddenly caught the ship, and of
the various expedients tried to escape destruction.
The longboat was hoisted and the ship was 'frapped'
or undergirt with cables passed beneath the hull[2].

passage he gives a list of the chief winds in the Mediterranean,
as follows :—

(1) ab oriente aequinoctiali 〔 from S.E. Subsolanus (Apeliotes).
    „   „   brumali   〔   „   N.E. Volturnus (Eurus).
                             〔   „   S. Auster.

(2) ab occasu brumali   from S. Africus (Notus-Liba).

(3) „   „   aequinoctiali   „   W. Favonius.

(4) „   „   solstitiali   „   N.W. Corus-Zephyrus. Ar-
                                           gestes.

(5) a septentrionibus.   Septentrio.

(6) inter eum (sc. Sept.) et 〕 Aquilo. Aparcties. Boreas.
    exortum solstitialem   〕

The steadiness of the Etesian winds in late summer was a
great obstacle to ships sailing from the east; in 70 they prevented
the news of Vespasian's successes reaching Vitellius (Meriv. VIII.
p. 122). Yet Pliny says that as they blew in the daytime only,
from the third hour, it was possible to progress, though slowly,
by sailing at night.

[1] Acts xxvii.

[2] These ὑποζώματα ('helps' E.V.) were, in the case of triremes,
fastened *horizontally* round the vessel to keep the timbers firm
under the constant strain from working the oars and from
ramming. But in the case of a merchant-ship what was wanted
was to keep the hull from being dashed to pieces by the storm;
for this purpose *vertical* ropes would be required.

The danger then arose of being driven on the terrible quicksands of the Syrtis; the great yard was lowered[1], and the ship was allowed to drift. The next day as a desperate remedy the ship was lightened, and the day after even the tackling was thrown overboard[2]. The ship drifted helplessly up and down 'in Adria' till it reached Melita; then after food had been served out to all on board, the precious cargo of wheat was thrown over, and at daybreak an attempt was made to land. No lives were lost, but the ship was completely wrecked. Elsewhere[3] we read of men cutting down the mast and even using outspread clothes for sails[4].

Doubtless on St Paul's ship there were many prayers offered to the Dioscuri, the sailors' gods, and many gifts vowed to Isis if life were granted. "Be mindful of God," says Epictetus, "call Him to be thy helper and defender as men call upon the Dioscuri in a storm[5]." Of such invocations we have an example in the Greek Anthology; Damis prays to the "queen of Egypt, goddess of the linen robe," to save him from the sea, and vows "even of his poverty" to sacrifice to her a deer with gilded horns[6]. We hear much of the votive pictures hung up in temples or carried about by shipwrecked

---

[1] Farrar, *St Paul*, Vol. ii. p. 374 (after Smith).

[2] Cf. Catullus in Juvenal, who sacrificed for dear life all his treasures; purple garments, silver plate, a chased dinner service once the property of Philip of Macedon.

[3] Juv. xii. 54—6.

[4] Juv. xii. 67.   Tac. ii. 24.   [5] *Ench.* 33.

[6] *Anth. Pal.* 6, 231.

men[1] to excite compassion. Those who could not
offer even a picture, offered their hair, as did
Lucillius in Lucian's epigram.

> " Poseidon and all Ocean deities
>   Lucillius, 'scaped from shipwreck on the seas,
>   Doth dedicate to you who bade him live
>   His hair, for nothing else is left to give[2]."

Such thank-offerings were well deserved, for
besides the dangers of the sea itself, sailors had
to fear wreckers[3] and pirates. The former were to
be found among the fishermen of the Cyclades, and
in the second century wrecking was forbidden by
frequent imperial edicts. Often the unfortunate
victims were sold as slaves. In the Euboean idyll
of Dio Chrysostom the countryman who is taken to
the town is accused by the mob orator of plundering
those wrecked off the dangerous Hollows of Euboea[4];
the charge is however disproved by the evidence of
a man who had been wrecked there and received
great kindness[4].

With regard to pirates the case seems to have *Piracy.*
been much the same as with brigands. On the
whole the Mediterranean was secure, if we may
believe Pliny, who speaks of the many thousands
of mariners who take advantage of the unbroken
peace[5]. So too Plutarch in his essay on ' Contented-

---

[1] Hor. *Car.* I. 5, *A. P.* 20, 21. Mart. XII. 57. Pers. I. 88—90,
VI. 32, 33.

[2] Anth. *Pal.* VI. 164, trans. by R. Garnett.

[3] Cf. Petron. ch. 114, procurrere piscatores parvulis expeditis
navigiis ad praedam rapiendam.

[4] Dio Chrys. *Or.* VII.   [5] Plin. *H. N.* II. 117.

ness of mind' reckons as one of the everyday
blessings of life that the sea is secure to mariners.
Strabo too in several passages writes to the same
effect[1].

Yet in distant seas pirates flourished still. Dio
Chrysostom[2] speaks of ransoming men captured by
pirates in a way that reminds us of the like good
deeds in the days of the Barbary corsairs. Seneca
too quotes as instances of cruelty the flogging and
burning alive by pirates of their captives[3]. The
precautions taken in the Indian Ocean against
piracy have been mentioned above[4]. In the Black
Sea much damage to trade was caused by barbarian
tribes who scoured the sea in vessels called 'camarae,'
constructed with high bulwarks to keep off the
waves in stormy weather, and a convertible arrangement of oars so that they could be paddled in either
direction[5]. Strabo says of these tribes that they
attacked merchant vessels and raided the coast,
often finding help from the Bosporani, who supplied
them with provisions and let them have a market
for their booty. In the winter their boats were
hauled ashore and hidden in the forests; they themselves kept in practice for the summer by highway
robbery[6]. Even in more frequented regions we
occasionally hear of pirates; after the Jewish revolt
of 66—70 A.D. a band established themselves in
Joppa and for a while stopped communication
between Syria and Egypt[7]. Nicarchus, who pro-

[1] Strab. III. 2, 145, and XI. 2, 12.   [2] Dio Chrys. XIV. 440 R.
[3] Sen. De Clem. II. ch. 4.   [4] P. 33.   [5] Tac. Hist. III. 47.
[6] Strab. XI. 2, 12.   [7] Josephus, B. J. III. 9, 2.

bably lived near the beginning of the second century, has the following poem in the Greek Anthology[1] :—

> " A starry seer's oracular abodes
> One sought, to know if he should sail for Rhodes,
> When thus the sage ' I rede thee, let thy ship
> Be new, and choose the summer for thy trip ;
> Safe then thou'lt leave, and safe regain this spot,
> If those confounded pirates catch thee not.' "

In spite of all hindrances the average speed of an ancient vessel which combined the use of oar and sail was quite as great as that of a modern vessel till the invention of steam-ships. Pliny gives the time for a voyage from Ostia to Gades as seven days, to Tarraco four days, Africa two, Forum Iulii three[2]. For a merchant ship of Alexandria to reach Massilia in thirty days was thought quick : from Messina Alexandria could be reached in six days : Narbo to Utica took five and Utica to Alexandria seven[3]. The average speed was therefore from a thousand to eighteen hundred stades in twenty-four hours, or about five nautical miles an hour for an ordinary, to seven and a half for a fast sailing ship[4].

Speed of sailing and rowing.

That sea travelling was general in the first century may be gathered, if from nothing else, from the illustrations and metaphors of rhetors and philosophers. For example, in twelve of Dio's orations no fewer than fifteen allusions occur to

[1] Trans. by R. Garnett.   Tomson's *Gk. Anthol.* p. 191.
[2] Plin. *H. N.* xix. 1.   [3] So Friedländer.
[4] Cf. Diod. Sic. iii. 34, from the Palus Maeotis to Rhodes took ten days with good winds, to Alexandria another four, thence up the Nile to Ethiopia ten more.

voyaging¹. Yet the sea is mentioned more often
than not with dread. This doubtless was due not
only to the actual perils thereon encountered, but to
the kind of literary tradition which makes Horace
sing of the 'estranging Ocean' and marvel at the
courage of the man,

> "Who in frail bark through surging waters first
>   With heart undaunted burst,
> Nor feared conflicting storms that lashed the seas
>   Or the sad portent of the Hyades²."

Here he repeats the idea, as old as Hesiod, that
'commerce and the mingling of nations are against
nature and a source of evil and would cease with
the return of the golden age³.' Hence tirades
against sea-travelling and restlessness need not be
taken too seriously, as for instance the familiar
lines :

> "Caelum non animum mutant qui trans mare currunt,
>   Strenua nos exercet inertia ; navibus atque
>   Quadrigis petimus bene vivere : Quod petis hic est,
>   Est Ulubris animus si te non deficit aequus⁴."

The first of these, untrue as it is, served as a
text for many philosophers. "He who thinks those
happy," Plutarch writes, "who are always scouring
the country and pass most of their time in inns and

---

¹ A few of these may be cited :—461 R, 471 R, 623 R, 14 R ɪɪ,
41 R ɪɪ, 49 R ɪɪ, 51 R ɪɪ, 136 R ɪɪ, 157 R ɪɪ, etc. etc. The point
is often the unity of will necessary on board ship as in 157 R ɪɪ,
and 240 R ɪɪ, or the skill necessary in a pilot as in 346 R ɪɪ.

² Hor. *Od.* ɪ. 3 (de Vere's translation).

³ Wickham on Hor. *Od.* ɪ. 3.   ⁴ Hor. *Epp.* ɪ. 11. 27—30.

ferry boats, is like a person who thinks the planets happier than the fixed stars [1]." And again in the same essay, where he extols the freedom of the exile from borrowers and duns, he says, " And a man not altogether silly or madly in love with crowds might I think not blame fortune for confining him to an island, but might even praise her for relieving him from weariness and anxiety and wanderings in foreign countries and perils by sea and the uproar of the forum [1]." His melancholy tone, in fact, reminds us of the sage who reckoned men at sea neither among the living nor the dead. We find nothing, in the classical writers of the Empire, like the fierce joy of the Viking; their odes were to the ' mild Favonius ' not the ' wild north-easter.' Neither were the Romans possessed with the passion of exploration : the elder Pliny complains that in former days, despite constant wars and piracy, the Greeks had eagerly sought the advancement of knowledge, but that in his day men only sailed to get gain. This may account perhaps for the strange fact that they failed to accomplish what was done by the Danes with far fewer resources, viz. the discovery of that Vinland, whose existence was soon forgotten again till the days of Vespucci and Columbus.

Nowhere perhaps is the restlessness and sadness of life on the sea felt more keenly than in the Greek Anthology. Many of these poems bewail the fate of those who have died at sea, and lost the tomb

---

[1] Plut. On Exile.

that might have kept their memory alive. Here
is one by Cicero's friend, Archias of Byzantium :

"Crushed by the waves upon the crag was I,
    Who still must hear these waves among the dead,
Breaking and brawling on the promontory,
    Sleepless ; and sleepless is my weary head.
For me did strangers bury on the coast
    Within the hateful hearing of the deep,
Nor death, that lulleth all, can lull my ghost,
    One sleepless soul among the souls that sleep[1]."

                                    ANDREW LANG.

Callimachus strikes a more passionate note in his
lament :

"Now would to God swift ships had ne'er been made !
Then, Sopolis, we had not mourned thy shade—
Dear son of Diocleides seaward sent !
Now somewhere in deep seas thy corse is tost
Hither and thither—and for whom we lost
We find thy name and empty monument[2]."

                                    WILLIAM HARDINGE.

With this, for the idea, though not for the grace of
expression, may be compared the wail of Ovid, which
is recalled in a stanza of *In Memoriam*[3] :

"Nec letum timeo ; genus est miserabile leti
    Demite naufragium : mors mihi munus erit.
Est aliquid, fatove suo ferrove cadentem
    In solida moriens ponere corpus humo[4]."

[1] Tomson's *Gk. Anthol.* p. 77.   [2] Ibid. p. 92.
[3] *In Memoriam* XVIII.

        "'Tis well ; 'tis something ; we may stand
            Where he in English earth is laid,
            And from his ashes may be made
        The violets of his native land."

[4] Ov. *Trist.* I. 2. 51—54.

Sometimes again there is no lament, only a prayer
that others may be more fortunate :

"Whose tomb I am, O mariner, do not thou ask of me,
   Only be it thy lot to find a less tempestuous sea[1]."
                              Trans. by ALMA STRETTELL.

Yet again, in a poem, characteristic of the Anthology
in its clinging to the 'pleasant light of the sun,' the
sailor envies the shepherd his life of peace :

"O happy swain, I would that unto me
   Who roamed rude ocean, the felicity
   Of shepherd's crook and carol had been known
   Ere yet I came a corpse by Eurus blown
   To these delightful shores where thou, most blest,
   Thy snowy flock serenely pasturest[2]."
                              R. GARNETT.

But it is time to turn from sea-voyages and *River and
lake
travelling.* their perils to the safe travelling by rivers, canals
and lakes.   Most important among navigable rivers
was of course the Tiber: as early as the foundation
of Rome commerce had gone up and down the
'yellow stream,' and in Livy's fifth book we read
that the produce of Latium was thus conveyed to
the sea.   Much effort was expended from time to
time in keeping the channel free from mud.   Under 15 A.D.
Tiberius 'curatores alvei et riparum Tiberis' were
appointed, who dredged the river and repaired the
embankment wall and the sewer mouths.   The river
was navigable from Trusiamnum in the territory of
Perusia; probably the inland commerce of the regions
bordering the Adriatic went through Ravenna up to
Pisaurum, then by waggons to Trusiamnum and so

---

[1] Tomson, p. 42.   [2] Ibid. p. 97.

by barges down the Tiber (Bergier). The produce
of Pliny's Tuscan estate, which was watered by the
Tiber, was conveyed down it to Rome in the winter
and spring: the chief article would of course be
wine from the Apennine vineyards[1]. Several of the
Tiber tributaries were also navigable, especially the
Nar. Tacitus relates that Piso on being summoned
home for trial after Germanicus' death, crossed the
Dalmatian Sea to Ancona, thence went through
Picenum along the Via Flaminia to Narnia, whence
he sailed down the Nar and the Tiber, landing at
the tomb of the Caesars[2]. Even the Umbrian
stream Clitumnus had its barges, which were carried
down by the strong current without need of oars[3].

Of far greater importance however was the traffic
up that river, which Pliny the elder in one of his
flights of rhetoric calls "rerum in toto orbe nascen-
tium mercator placidissimus[4]." Usually large vessels
unloaded their cargoes into barges, while small ones
were lightened and towed up[5]. Especially important were the barges and landing-places for the
marble blocks, of which great quantities were brought
to Rome. At the foot of the Aventine was the old
'Marmoratum' of which remains still exist. These
are a number of huge unsculptured travertine
corbels (8 feet long by 3 feet deep), each pierced

[1] Juv. vii. 121, vinum Tiberi devectum.
[2] Tac. *Ann.* iii. 9.   [3] Plin. *Epp.* viii. 88.
[4] Plin. *H. N.* v. 3 § 53.
[5] The noise of the bargees and the shouts of the steersman
giving the "time" to the crew are counted by Martial among the
disagreeables of city life, Mart. iv. 64.

with a hole to receive the hawsers of the ships
fastened here whilst discharging their cargoes of
marble blocks[1]. The extensive buildings in the
Campus Martius under Augustus made a new
marble wharf necessary, if a troublesome journey
through the streets from the Aventine was to be
avoided. The new one, of which the remains have
been recently discovered, was about 175 yards above
the Pons Aelius, now the Bridge of St Angelo, and
dates probably from the time of Augustus.

In this connexion may be mentioned also the
vast store-houses for foreign imports of all descriptions which stretched for a mile along the Tiber
bank mingled with bakers' shops and corn-mills.
The chief was the Horrea Galbea et Aniciana at
the foot of the Aventine near the landing quay of
the Tiber. It consisted of a series of open courts
surrounded by chambers two floors high for storage
purposes. In the same region of the city five other
store-houses are known to have existed; while in
312 A.D. the total number for Rome is given as 290.
Professor Lanciani during recent explorations in the
Horrea Galbea found in the various store-chambers
a motley collection of articles, including lentils, sand
for sawing marble, amphorae, and a mass of elephants'
tusks[2]. The granaries covered a large area, as is
shown by the vast amount imported every year—
144 million bushels even under Augustus, when the
city population was under two millions. The scholiast
on Lucan I. 319 says that in his time 80,000 modii

---

[1] Middleton, I. p. 148.
[2] Lanc. *Anc. Rome*, p. 250.

were daily consumed in Rome: Septimus Severus
kept enough to last seven years.

Perhaps the most striking proof of the vastness
of the Tiber traffic is the so-called Monte Testaccio.
This is composed of fragments of pottery, mainly
from amphorae in which goods of all kinds were
brought to Rome. According to Lanciani a space
was reserved for the bits of broken amphorae and
the accumulations of centuries have resulted in
a hill 160 feet high, covering an area of 16 acres.

With regard to the other rivers of the Empire
we have no such details as for the Tiber, but there
is no doubt that they were extensively used for
communication. The route from Ravenna to Altinum
has been mentioned already; no doubt there was
barge and boat traffic on the river itself as well as
on the lagoons near its mouth. Especially in Gaul
was river communication frequent; even before the
conquest "the tolls of the river and maritime
ports played a great part in the budget of certain
cantons[1]." It was quite possible to traverse Gaul
from north to south by the rivers with the exception
of some few miles between the Sequana (Seine) and
the Arar (Saône)[2]. In Egypt up to the First
Cataract the Nile was the easiest route and was
the scene of busy traffic. From scarcity of wood,
other materials for boats had been adopted. Often
they were made of reed, papyrus or rush, a custom
as old as the Book of Job, where the 'swift ships'

[1] Mommsen, Vol. IV. p. 220.
[2] Strab. IV. 1. 14.

are literally 'ships of reed[1].' Several allusions also
occur to earthenware boats, the brightly coloured
phaseli mentioned by Vergil and Juvenal[2]. Strabo[3]
during his visit to Egypt was surprised at the slowness of these makeshifts. The modern reader is
likely to be surprised rather at the marvellous
variety in the means of communication over the
vast area which formed the Empire.

Closely connected with river traffic is that *Traffic on*
carried on by canals and lakes. The age saw many *canals and lakes.*
great projects and some great performances in the
way of canals. Julius Caesar and afterwards Gaius
planned the piercing of the Isthmus of Corinth[4],
but the attempt came to nothing. Another unsuc-
cessful venture was Nero's projected canal from
Lake Avernus to the mouth of the Tiber, which
would have required immense outlay and labour
for inadequate results[5]. Among more useful enter-
prises may be reckoned the Fossa Drusiana, connecting the Rhine with the Zuyder Zee (then Lake
Flevo). This was constructed by the elder Drusus
in 12 B.C. Equally useful for military purposes was
Corbulo's canal between the Meuse and the Rhine.
A third plan, which would have been of great
commercial benefit, was quashed through jealousy
of its author. L. Vetus, one of the legati of
Germany, proposed in 59 A.D. to connect the

---

[1] Job ix. 26. Cf. Juv. v. 89. Plin. *H. N.* vii. § 206. Lucan,
Phars. iv. 136.
[2] Verg. *Georg.* iv. 287—9. Juv. xv. 126.
[3] Strab. p. 788.   [4] Suet. *Iul.* 44; *Cal* 21.
[5] Tac. *Ann.* xv. 43.

Moselle and the Saône (Arar) so that communication
between the Mediterranean and the North Sea
might be entirely by water, viz. along the Rhone,
the Saône, Moselle and Rhine. The neighbouring
legatus of Belgica condemned the plan as contrary
to imperial policy[1]. A canal much used was that
connecting Canopus[2] with Alexandria, which was
covered with boats containing the idlest and most
vicious pleasure-seekers of the Empire. The con-
course passed into a proverb, as we see from Seneca,
who writes : " The wise man, or he who aims at
becoming so, must avoid certain abodes as unfavour-
able to virtuous practice. Therefore if he be looking
about for a quiet retreat, he will not choose Canopus[3]."
This canal was only one of a network which covered
a large part of Egypt for irrigation as well as for
transit purposes.

With regard to communication by lakes we have
few details, except for the Sea of Galilee, which as
is shown in the Gospels was the usual way of connexion between Galilee and Decapolis. We may
be sure that, wherever possible, lakes were utilized.
An instance may be quoted from Pliny's letter to
Trajan describing a lake of considerable size near
Nicomedia, on which marble, corn, logs, etc. were
easily conveyed. Pliny suggests the continuation
of this water-traffic to the sea by making a
canal.

The merchants of the Empire had discovered
the comparative cheapness of water-traffic, and the

---

[1] Tac. *Ann.* XIII. 53.   [2] Strab. 800, 801.
[3] Sen. *Ep.* 51 § 3.   Mayor, Vol. I. p. 98.

State and private individuals were not behindhand.
Beyond doubt the transporting of soldiers was
carried on as far as possible by water, and sea-
voyages were for most men less fatiguing than
land-journeys[1]. During the short season of navigation the Mediterranean was crowded to such
an extent that Juvenal can bid his readers 'look
at the harbours and the sea covered with ships;
more men are now afloat than ashore[2].' Prof. Mayor
in commenting on this passage points out that what
is now done by letter or cable had then to be done
by personal visits. The merchant of the first
century well deserved to be called by Horace
'unwearied'; there were doubtless not a few who
could, like Flavius Zeuxis, have it recorded on
their tomb that they had sailed seventy-two times
round Malea into Italy[3].

---

[1] Cf. Tac. *Hist.* i. 33.

[2] Juv. xv. 275.

[3] *C. I. G.* 3920.   Φλάουιος Ξεῦξις ἐργαστὴς πλεύσας ὑπὲρ Μαλέαν
εἰς Ἰταλίαν πλόας ἑβδομήκοντα δύο.

CHAPTER V.

COMMUNICATION IN ASIA MINOR.

THE foregoing sketch, inadequate as it is, shows first, that the provinces and Rome were during the first century in constant communication, secondly, that travellers enjoyed greater security than ever before and greater than in many centuries after, and thirdly, that no satisfactory account of the system of communication in a country can be given without a full knowledge of its geography, history, and social conditions. Such knowledge, is for the first century, imperfect indeed, though a mass of literature has come down to us. Mommsen[1] is indignant at the 'telling of what deserved to be suppressed, and the suppression of what there was need to tell.' Still one generation can never look at itself with the eyes of another; unless for the benefit of posterity it seems hardly worth while to write what everybody knows. Hence there are woeful gaps in our knowledge, which however, it is to be hoped, may be filled up partly by fresh epigraphic evidence.

[1] *Provinces of the Roman Empire*, Introd. Vol. I.

It remains to fill up this outline of the system *Asia* of communication in the case of Asia Minor. More *Minor.* *Physical* than in many countries this was determined by *features.* physical conditions. The region west of the Tigris to the Levant consists for the most part of a plateau whose mean elevation varies from 3500 to 4000 feet above sea-level, stretching for about 200 miles with an average breadth of 140 miles. Bordering this plateau south and north are two broken mountain ranges which branch out from the Armenian uplands. The southern, or Taurus, range begins near the Euphrates and continues in a general westerly direction to the Aegean, sending out spurs to the north and south at various points. The average height ranges from 7000 to 10,000 or even 13,000 feet : in character the chain is rugged and intersected by many chasms and ravines. There are but few passes and those snow-covered till May or June. The Anti-Taurus range runs in two or three parallel chains close to the Euxine as far as the Bosporus. Thence it throws off southern spurs, the chief being Mt Ida and the Mysian Olympus. Several branches also run into the interior : the highest peak in these and in the whole peninsula is Mount Argaeus (Ergish dagh), over 13,000 feet in height. On the north the mountains are at a very short distance from the sea ; on the south there is a coast plain rising abruptly to the central plateau ; on the west are a number of river valleys (Caicus, Hermus, Maeander), separated by spurs of the Taurus which jut out into the Aegean.

The rivers on the south are short and rapid,

liable to floods in winter, while in the summer their
volume is much diminished. The largest rivers of
the peninsula are the Halys and Sangarius, flowing
into the Euxine. A remarkable feature of the
plateau is the number of fresh and salt water lakes,
the chief being Lake Tatta, some sixty miles north
of Konia (Iconium). Of the fresh water lakes the
largest is the Egerdir (the ancient Limnae) in the
Pisidian mountains. The region round Lake Tatta
is practically desert, as the rainfall is small and un-
certain. The climate of the plateau generally is
sultry in summer and cold in winter, snow lying
deep on the ground for four months. The western
and southern coasts present a great contrast with
their warm but not oppressive summers and their
cooling sea-breezes[1].

The soil of the peninsula is naturally very rich:
in the valleys, even after centuries of neglect, fruits
of all kinds and cereals are grown in abundance; the
soil needs only to be scratched to be productive.
The Taurus slopes are in many places clothed with
pines and firs, and the upland districts, especially
towards the Euphrates, afford good pasturage. In
imperial times, when the land was carefully cultivated, Asia Minor was one of the richest countries
of the world. There were many sources of wealth
besides agriculture; the great cities on the Aegean
coast were important manufacturing centres; productive marble quarries were to be found at Dorylaeum
and purple fisheries off Miletus.

[1] The Pamphylian plain however had a bad climate, malaria
being frequent, as is the case to-day.

This sketch of the natural features of the country
gives some clue to the general character of its system
of communication. Given a country with two roughly
parallel mountain ranges running east and west and
a desert in the centre of the enclosed plateau, it is
clear that traffic must necessarily set east and west
either north or south of this desert. The position
of Asia Minor relatively to surrounding countries
shows further that it must always have served to
connect the East with the West. To quote Prof.
Ramsay, " Planted like a bridge between Asia and
Europe, the peninsula of Asia Minor has been from
the beginning of history a battlefield between the
East and the West. Across this bridge the religion,
art and civilization of the East found their way into
Greece ; and the civilization of Greece under the
guidance of Alexander the Macedonian passed back
again across the same bridge to conquer the East
and revolutionize Asia as far as the heart of India.
Persians, Arabs, Mongols, Turks, have all followed
the same route in the many attempts that Asia has
made to subdue the West[1]."

This conflict between the Oriental and European *Civilisa-*
spirit accounts for the fact that in the first century *tion.*
A.D. the inhabitants of Asia Minor varied widely in
race and civilization. Greek influence, which had
begun on the north and west coasts in the early days
of colonization, had been extended to the interior
under Alexander and the successors, and later under
the kings of Pergamus. A fresh element had been

[1] *Hist. Geog. of Asia Minor*, p. 23 (referred to henceforth as
H. G. A. M.).

introduced by the Gallic invasions of the third century B.C. and the settlement in the district henceforward known as Gallograecia or Galatia. The Romans appeared in Asia Minor as the extenders of Hellenism : the urban foundations of the Seleucids and Attalids increased in population and wealth till men could speak of " the province of the five hundred towns." In spite of the disasters suffered in the third Mithradatic war, there was, during the first century of our era, a high degree of prosperity. Here as elsewhere the imperial rule was for the provincials an unmixed benefit. The remains of aqueducts, theatres and temples show to this day the diffusion of wealth throughout the country ; as an instance may be cited the ruins of the Lycian town of Cragus-Sidyma, of which Mommsen says, " In the whole Vilayet Aidin there is at the present day no inland place which can be even remotely placed by the side of this little mountain-town, such as it was then as regards civilised existence[1]."

In the urban life three features are especially noticeable: the petty rivalries of the cities, which are severely ridiculed by Dio of Prusa[2] as " Greek follies "; the splendour and frequency of the spectacles, athletic and musical contests, and festivals of all descriptions ; and lastly the high development of the system of κοινά answering to the provincial councils of the West. The Asiarchs, Bithyniarchs, and so forth, were high priests of the temple where the emperor was worshipped, and conducted the festivals in his

[1] Mommsen, *Provinces of the Roman Empire*, vol. I. p. 356.
[2] Dio Chrys. xxvII. 528 R.

honour. Their position was much sought after on
account of its outward magnificence, and they seem
to have formed something like a nobility of office.

With regard to political relations with Rome, *Govern-*
the geographical area now known as Asia Minor was *ment.*
in the first century divided into a number of provinces, partly imperial, partly senatorial. To the
former class, under proconsuls elected by lot for one
year, belonged first, Asia[1] in the official sense,
including the old districts of Mysia, Lydia, and
Caria, bequeathed to the Roman people by Attalus
III., the last king of Pergamus. Next came
Bithynia-Pontus, gained partly by bequest from
Nicomedes, king of Bithynia, partly by conquest
from Mithradates Eupator. Third[2] came Cyprus
and Cyrene, each bequeathed by its last ruler to the
people of Rome, and lastly Crete, occupied by
Metellus as a base against the pirates. Under
direct imperial administration were various territories, mostly acquired during the first century.

[1] The boundaries of Asia are thus given by Prof. Ramsay
(*H. G. A. M.* p. 171). Beginning with the north the line ran
up the Rhyndacus, beyond Hadriani, then east, keeping north of
Dorylaion, then south, keeping east of Accylaion, Trocnades,
Orcistos, and Philomelion; south of Hadrianopolis, N.W. along
the Sultan Dagh, not including Neapolis and Antioch, then S.W.
along a ridge to the valley of Dombai, then south, the boundary
being marked between Apollonia and Apameia by a stone still
preserved; then S.W. through L. Ascania, between Lysinia and
Tymbrianassos, and between Olbasa and the Ormeleis; south
along the upper waters of the Lysis, W. through L. Caralitis and
along the Indos to the sea. (See also the maps in *H. G. A. M.*
and in *Cities and Bishoprics.*)

[2] These were always reckoned with Asia Minor.

The largest was the province of Galatia, which varied much in extent at different epochs. Towards the middle of the first century A.D., the time of St Paul's journeys, it comprised the following districts :—Galatia proper, bequeathed by king Amyntas in 25 B.C., Pisidia, Lycaonia, Paphlagonia, Pontus Galaticus, and small districts of Phrygia and Isauria[1]. The kingdom of Cappadocia was added to the Empire in 17 A.D. and the Lycian city confederation in 43 A.D. Under Nero in 63 A.D. the north-eastern frontier was extended from the valley of the Iris to Armenia, while under Vespasian were annexed Lesser Armenia and some smaller districts in Cilicia.

Road-system. The Romans did not originate the road-system any more than the city life of Asia Minor: both have a long history, the beginning of which is lost in the mists of the past. In the pre-Persian epoch it seems that a road from the Euphrates led north of the salt lake region through Pteria to Sardis and Ephesus; Pteria was connected too with Sinope on the Euxine. This road is difficult and circuitous, and owed its origin in all probability to the fact that Pteria was the metropolis of a great empire. The Persians adopted the same route under the name of the Royal Road described by Herodotus. In course of time when the greatness of Pteria had been utterly forgotten, intercourse naturally followed the easier route, viz., that to the south of the great desert. Hence between 300 and 100 B.C. the great

[1] *H. G. A. M.* p. 254.

trade route came into use, the result "of the
gradual penetration of commerce and intercourse,
pushing on the one hand west from the Cilician
Gates, and on the other hand east from the
Maeander and Lycus valleys[1]."

The Romans naturally adopted the route that *The great
trade
route.*
had been worked out under the Greek kings and
made it the backbone of their system. As in other
provinces, their object was quick communication
with Rome, hence the chief highway terminated
at Ephesus, whence Rome could be reached either
by sea or by land and sea combined. Ephesus, as the
de facto capital[2] of Asia and the residence of the
proconsul, was the chief city of the whole peninsula.
It had extensive docks and a fine harbour, Panormus.
The engineer employed by Attalus Philadelphus had
built a mole which kept in the mud brought down
by the Cayster, ultimately ruining the harbour; but
as yet the commercial supremacy of the city
remained unshaken. Important manufactures had
their seat at Ephesus, *e.g.* the silver shrines made by
Demetrius and his fellows for the worshippers of the
Ephesian Artemis. Religion indeed as well as
commerce attracted crowds to the city; the great
temple of the Nature-goddess, identified with the
Greek Artemis, was celebrated throughout the
world. On its completion, according to the legend,
Mithradates had granted a right of asylum extending
round it as far as a bowshot; by a miracle the
arrow flew a furlong's distance. Naturally criminals

[1] *H. G. A. M.* p. 38.
[2] Pergamus was the official capital of the province of Asia.

and scoundrels of all descriptions flocked to the
neighbourhood of the temple, till Tiberius in the inte-
rests of public order restricted the bounds. On Mt
Solmissus, where there were many other temples,
a panegyric festival was held annually at which the
mystic rites of the Curetes were celebrated[1]. In
fact the Ephesians passed their life amid the frantic
worship of the mother of the gods, varied by the
celebration of Panionic, Ephesian, or Artemisian
Games[2].

The great road from Ephesus to the East is
given in the Peutinger Table in only a fragmentary
form ; its existence is proved by Strabo, who speaks
of a road from Ephesus to Antioch and the Maeander.
The first great town it passed was Magnesia, south-
east of Ephesus ; to the east of this was Tralles,
celebrated in Strabo's time for its wealth and for the
number of its citizens who attained the dignity of
Asiarch[3]. The next important place was Antioch
ad Maeandrum, where the road crossed the river by
a bridge[4], probably constructed by M'. Aquillius in
129 B.C. when he laid out the roads of the province
of Asia. It consisted of six arches and is often
represented on coins of Antioch. Keeping still due
east the road passed through Carura, noted for its
number of inns used by visitors to the hot baths, and
then reached Laodicea, which is situated on a small
plateau raised above the lowlands along the Lycus.

---

[1] Strab. xiv. 1.

[2] The luxury of Ephesus is probably depicted in the 18th
chapter of the Apocalypse, especially vv. 11—17.

[3] Strab. 648.   [4] Ibid. 630.

This river-valley is the easiest approach from the
coast region to the great central plateau, and during
the Greek and Roman periods it was the main
artery of communication[1]. The city, named after
his wife Laodice, had been founded by Antiochus II.
(261—246 B.C.) to strengthen his hold on the district
by means of Macedonian colonists. In Strabo's time
its prosperity had greatly increased; the territory
afforded pasturage for the glossy black sheep whose
wool was woven into fine cloth, carpets and garments. The latter are referred to in the letter
to the Church of Laodicea:—" I counsel thee to
buy of me (not the glossy *black* garments of
Laodicea, but) *white* garments that thou mayest
clothe thyself[2]."

From the Syrian gate of Laodicea the road passed
along the glen of the Upper Lycus to Colossae, which
was built originally on the southern bank, though it
had extended to the northern also. Commercially
it had been ruined by the foundation of Laodicea,
only ten miles away. Strabo calls it a small town,
though in the fifth century B.C. it had been " a
populous city, prosperous and great." Its dark
purple wool was almost as much valued as that
of Laodicea, but the town would now scarcely be
remembered but for the connexion with St Paul.
After leaving Colossae the road ascended steadily,
yet gently, to the plateau, passed the Bitter Salt
Lake (Anava) and turned north-east till it reached
Apamea. This, like Laodicea, was a Seleucid foun-

---

[1] Ramsay, *Cities and Bishoprics*, p. 5.
[2] Rev. iii. 18; *Cities and Bishoprics*, p. 42.

dation, built by Antiochus Soter, and peopled with
the inhabitants of the ancient city of Celaenae hard
by. It was according to Strabo the busiest place
in the province of Asia after Ephesus, being an
entrepôt for those coming from Greece and Italy.

Leaving Apamea the eastern highway bore past
Metropolis, Euphorbium, and Julia to Philomelium,
and then turned south-east to Laodicea (κατακεκαυμένη), so called to distinguish it from Laodicea
ad Lycum. Now keeping due east it traversed the
bare plateau of Lycaonia, past Savatra and Coro-
passus, and then through Cappadocia, past Archelais
to Caesarea Mazaca. This town under its old name
of Mazaca had been the capital of Cappadocia: it
received its name of Caesarea on the annexation of
the country under Tiberius. Near it was Mt Argaeus,
the highest mountain of the peninsula, the top of
which was always covered with snow. Strabo notes
that in a clear sky a view can be gained from it to
the Euxine on the north and the Sinus Issicus to
the south, but that very few have been on the
summit. He adds further that the city of Mazaca
had been purposely left unwalled lest the inhabitants
should take to brigandage. Thence the route kept
due east, passing various important military stations,
till it reached Melitene, the head-quarters of the
frontier defence system and the standing camp of
the Legio XII Fulminata. From Melitene a caravan
route crossed the Euphrates near Domisa to Armenia.

Branches of the great trade route. For the sake of clearness no branches of this
great road have yet been mentioned, but every
place of any importance along its course was a

'knot' where various side routes came in. First of all, from Ephesus, the starting point, a road ran on the left bank of the Cayster for about twenty-five miles, then crossed, and continued in a general north-easterly direction over Mt. Tmolus to Sardis. Another crossed the Cayster close to Ephesus, went north-east to Dios Hieron, then north-north-west to Smyrna. Hence was a twofold connexion with Sardis: the direct one through Nymphaeum and Sosandra, the circuitous one following the Hermus past Magnesia. From this second route branched the coast road through Cyme, Myrina, Elaea to Adramyttium, whence two roads led to Cyzicus on the Propontis. The direct one was north-east along the line of the river Aesepus, the other followed round the coast through Assos, Troas, Abydos and Lampsacus till it reached Cyzicus. Pergamus, the official capital of the province, was connected with the western coast at Elaea, at Atarneus and Adramyttium, with the Propontis at Cyzicus, and with Sardis through Germe; Nacrasa and Thyatira. From the last-named city a north road ran through Hadrianoutherae, joining the route from Pergamus and Cyzicus.

The first great knot after leaving Ephesus was Laodicea ad Lycum. Here met the road from the Pamphylian port of Attalia, that from Sardis through Philadelphia and Hierapolis, and from Phrygia through Brouzos, Eumenia, Peltae and Lounda.

From Apamea a road ran east to the Pisidian Antioch and another north-east to Synnada, Docimium and Amorium. Commercially this route was most

important for by it came the marble quarried two
or three miles from Docimium. The fact that this
marble was known as Synnadic leads to the sup-
position that at Synnada was situated "the chief
office of administration, to which orders for the
marble were sent[1]." North Phrygia was connected
with Apamea through Dorylaeum, Nacolea, Hierapolis and Eucarpia.

For the mountainous region south of Apamea
the centre of communication was Antioch, called
Pisidian to distinguish it from the more famous
Syrian Antioch on the Orontes[2]. Under the Republic the Roman power had never been secure on
the Pamphylian coast or in the Pisidian mountains.
The subjugation of the robber tribes was entrusted
by M. Antonius to the Galatian officer Amyntas,
who soon became King of Galatia and extended his
power over Lycaonia, Pisidia, Isauria, Pamphylia
and western Cilicia[3]. Up to his death in B.C. 25 he
did much to extirpate brigands and suppress piracy.
Later on we find that Antipater, the ruler of Derbe
and Laranda, drove the Pisidians out of southern
Phrygia, but was killed in an expedition against
the Homonadenses. This untoward event compelled
Augustus to take action. Pamphylia was placed
under a governor of its own: western Cilicia was
placed under Cappadocia, with the understanding
that the prince of the latter district should help

---

[1] *H. G. A. M.* p. 54.

[2] Its full description at the time of St Paul's visits would have
been, "a Phrygian city on the side of Pisidia."

[3] Mommsen, *Provinces*, I. ch. 8.

to pacify it; the remainder of Amyntas' dominions formed the new province of Galatia.

The policy of coercion was vigorously carried out on the usual Roman lines. About B.C. 6 a number of roads were made connecting the colonies of Antioch, Olbasa, Comana, Cremna, Parlais and Lystra[1]. The distances were probably counted from Antioch, as the number of miles stated on a milestone found on the site of Comana exactly corresponds with that given in the Peutinger Table between Antioch and Comana *viâ* Apollonia. The importance of Antioch continued for nearly three-quarters of a century till the mountaineers were incorporated in the Empire. Scattered notices in Tacitus show that this was no easy task. We read that the Syrian army had once to be called in to chastise the Homonadenses; that their territory was invaded and laid waste by P. Sulpicius Quirinus[2], who distributed the old inhabitants among the surrounding townships. In this connexion may be mentioned also the Clitae of western Cilicia, who when placed under Archelaus refused to submit to census and tribute, and held out against his forces on the heights of Mount Taurus. More than four thousand troops from Syria were needed to reduce them by sword and famine[3]. Undaunted, they repeated the same tactics in A.D. 53, making raids on the coast cities or committing piracy on trading vessels. Once more a Syrian force was sent, composed however of cavalry, who from the nature of the

---

[1] C. I. L. III. Supp. 6974, Rushforth, pp. 22—4.

[2] Tac. *Ann.* III. 48.   [3] Tac. *Ann.* VI. 44.

ground were unable to act. The commander was reduced to employ bribes and treachery to bring them to submission[1].

These roads branching from Antioch are especially noteworthy as exceptions to the general rule that communication in Asia Minor was for trading purposes.

Returning to the eastern highway, the next knot was Laodicea Combusta (κατακεκαυμένη), whence roads ran south to Iconium and north-west to Dorylaeum. Iconium was a centre for the roads of Lycaonia and Cilicia. It was connected with Tarsus by a road over the Taurus through the pass of the Cilician Gates, then so narrow that a loaded camel could only just pass between the rocky walls[2]. From a military point of view this pass has always been the most important in Asia Minor. At the northern entrance was the town of Tyana, which had direct communication with Iconium, as had also Lystra and Isauria. Further, from the port of Seleucia on the Calycadnus a road ran from Selinus to Rossus. Besides the Gates other passes led over Anti-Taurus, direct from Lycaonia to the Cilician coast, the most used being that leading viâ Andrasus to Celenderis.

For Cappadocia the road-knots were Archelais and Caesarea. At Archelais four roads met the eastern highway:—from Tyana through Nazianzus and so ultimately from Tarsus; from Tavium in North Galatia through Mocissus; from Ancyra through Parnassus on the Halys, and lastly from

---

[1] Tac. Ann. XII. 55.   [2] H. G. A. M. p. 58.

the old Galatian capital Pessinus. Caesarea was an even more important centre, for to it converged the roads over Anti-Taurus either from Cocussus and Comana[1], a road frequented at the present time, or from Arabissus and Ptanadaris, still of some importance and practicable for wheeled traffic[2]. Sebastia to the north-east and Tavium to the north-west also had direct connexion with Caesarea.

Melitene, the last knot, had a military importance similar to, though far greater than, that of the Pisidian Antioch. It was the centre of the roads guarding the frontier of the Empire towards the Euphrates. A road which roughly followed the course of the great river ran from Satala, the station of Legio XV Apollinaris through Arauraca and Dascusa to Melitene and thence to Samosata (the modern Samsat) in the province of Syria. Melitene was connected with the passes over Taurus by a road to Arabissus and Cocussus. From the last named a road ran through Comana to Sebastia and thence along the Halys to Nicopolis and Satala. This set of roads formed roughly an ellipse, the chief points on the circumference being Satala, Melitene, Arabissus and Sebastia; the two latter were connected by cross roads with Melitene, and from Germanicea due south of Arabissus two roads diverged to the Euphrates at Samosata and Zeugma, whence lay the caravan routes to Edessa.

This great route and its branches furnished the means of communication for Asia, southern Galatia,

---

[1] The emporium for the Armenian trade.   Strab. XII. 3, § 35.
[2] Ibid. p. 271.

Lycaonia, Cilicia and Cappadocia. There remains to be described the road-system of the north in Bithynia, northern Galatia, Pontus, and its connexion with the main route from Ephesus.

Northern road. The backbone of this northern system is a road running eastwards corresponding to the eastern highway. It started from Nicomedia, the northern Ephesus, as it were, and was united with the southern route by branches from Dorylaeum and Ancyra. Dorylaeum was the meeting point of the Phrygian roads, being connected with Apamea and Philadelphia to the south. Ancyra was the centre of the north Galatian system; it was linked with the eastern highway by a road to Parnassus forking to Archelais and to Mazaca; with Amasia and Amisus by Gangra and Euchaeta; lastly Amasia was connected with Comana Pontica and with Sebastia.

The above-mentioned road from Nicomedia through Nicaea, Dorylaeum, Ancyra, Archelais, Tyana, to Tarsus became one of the most important in Asia Minor when Constantinople was the capital of the Empire and all roads no longer 'led to Rome.' It was then used by pilgrims to the Holy Land, and was therefore constantly described. Even now considerable trade passes along it.

Before leaving the subject of the road-system of Asia Minor it may be well, even at the risk of repetition, to summarize its leading features. In the first place, the roads were trade routes with the exception of those radiating from Antioch and Melitene. Hence they were not made with such elaborate care as in other parts of the Empire, Italy especially.

Secondly, they preferred ease to straightness and were adapted when possible to the line of rivers and mountains. Thirdly, the main routes ran west and east, the skeleton of the system being as follows :— a highway from Ephesus to Melitene, sending out branches northwards to a roughly parallel road (Nicomedia to Satala) and southwards to the coast. Lastly, the road-system was very complete, as is obvious from the large number of cities existing in the country in the first century A.D.

The truth of this last statement is more clearly realized by comparing the communications of Asia Minor at the present time and nineteen hundred years ago. The unanimous evidence of travellers is that the country is infinitely worse off now than it was then. A passage from Prof. Ramsay's *Impressions of Turkey* is so much to the point that its length may be pardoned. " Though occasionally one finds a good new road built by some European in the Government service, the great majority of the roads which have been made in recent years in Asia Minor are bad. In more cases than one the line of the new road was indicated to our eyes by the deeper green of a more luxuriant crop of grass; the natives carefully avoided it because its surface was not so good for the horses' feet, and the track which they followed kept away from the road, only cutting across it occasionally. It is quite common to find an isolated piece of modern road without beginning or end. It is still commoner to find an elevated causeway, built at great expense, leading to the bank of a ravine or stream in preparation for a bridge ; but the bridge

has never been built.......When a new road is projected an entirely new line is selected, often one that
requires engineering works of some magnitude;
scraps of the road are made by forced labour; a
certain amount of money is spent, three times as
much money is embezzled by officials of various
ranks: then the whole enterprise is abandoned." M.
Perrot, some years earlier, wrote[1] :— " Whenever by
some lucky chance the traveller does find a bridge
or causeway, he nearly always has to thank the
builders of Roman or Byzantine times. In the East
the generations of to-day live off the remnants and,
if the expression may be used, the crumbs of the
past." Mr Hogarth found that the high road from
Konia (Iconium) was severely left alone, being grass-
grown, with rotten bridges, and often disconnected
from the embankments[2].

Safety of travelling. With regard to the safety of travellers the
contrast between now and then is not so strongly
marked. The police arrangements of the Empire
were by no means its strong point, and in Asia Minor
several causes contributed to make travelling rather
insecure. The mountainous nature of the country
was a direct incentive to brigandage, which went on
unchecked till the days of the Empire. Strabo gives
in some detail the story of the robber-chief Cleon,
who lived in a strong castle called Callydium, near
Gordium; by attacking those who were collecting
money for Labienus, governor of Asia, he rendered
considerable service to M. Antonius, but basely

[1] *Exploration archéologique*, Vol. I. p. 1.
[2] *Wandering Scholar*, p. 36.

deserted him for Octavian at the battle of Actium. His treachery was rewarded, inappropriately enough, with the priesthood of 'Zeus Abrettenos,' the god of the Mysians, and with a part of Morena in Mysia by way of territory. He also received a priesthood at Comana Pontica, where he shocked his colleagues by sacrificing pigs according to the custom of Lydia and Phrygia. Within a month he was smitten with disease and died, the priests at Comana attributing his end to the wrath of the goddess.

The peace which prevailed in the country on the establishment of the Principate put a stop to such flagrant crimes as those committed under the Republic, but the laxity of the senatorial administration, coupled with the fact that many cities possessed powers of self-government within their own territories, and in some cases rights of asylum as well, tended to make brigandage a profitable means of livelihood. In some districts even military force could not stamp out robbers; in spite of Augustus's efforts they continued in the Pisidian mountains. St Paul, in the description of what he had undergone during his journeys, mentions "perils of robbers," thinking doubtless of the journey from Pamphylia to Pisidian Antioch. A number of inscriptions[1] found near the site of Antioch show the extreme insecurity that prevailed. Thus an epitaph is erected by Patroklos and Douda over the grave of their son Sousou, slain by robbers. Another refers to armed policemen (ὀροφύλακες and παραφυλακῖται), and a third to a

---

[1] Ramsay, *St Paul the Traveller*, &c. p. 23.

stationarius, whose duty it was to catch runaway slaves turned brigands.

Now-a-days brigandage usually has a place in accounts of travel through Asia Minor. Thus Mr Hogarth in his *Wandering Scholar in the Levant* writes, "We have climbed three thousand feet and the waggon is drawn aside for the night by a little spring in a hidden hollow; the spot is chosen to escape the highwaymen who patrol the road[1]" Later on he says that the armed shepherds near the coast are often potential robbers if they see the odds to be clearly in their favour, and refers to the case of Mr Macmillan, who was killed on the Mysian Olympus in 1888. On the whole however it seems that there is no general sympathy with the brigands and that a little timely severity can make a province safe. In fact, the inhabitants of the plateau are so miserably poor that there is nothing for robbers to take.

Communication by sea and rivers. Passing from the road-system to communication by water we find that in some districts this was much easier than by land, *e.g.* on the northern coast. The Cyreian soldier Antileon told his comrades at Trapezus that he was weary of marching, and now that the sea was before him he longed to sail the rest of the way, and "arrive in Greece outstretched and asleep like Odysseus[2]." Such communication was even more tempting on the western coast with its numerous indentations and good harbours. Strabo, it may be remarked, in his description of Ionia, gives the distances from city to city by sea as

[1] Pp. 53, 54.
[2] Xen. *Anab.* v. 1, 3—13.

well as by land. His details as to harbours are
worth quoting ; Panormus at Ephesus has been
mentioned already ; Smyrna, which in later times
succeeded to the importance of Ephesus, had a
harbour that could be closed (κλειστὸς λιμήν) ; so
had Rhodes and Chios, the latter possessing also
a roadstead (ναύσταθμος) for eighty ships, and
several good anchorages. Samos had a roadstead,
Icaria anchorages, Teos and Erythrae harbours.
On the north coast were the harbours of Cyzicus,
Heraclea Pontica, Sinope and Amisus. Sinope had
lost the importance of its early days when it was the
harbour for the Cappadocian trade. A relic of this
period is to be found in the name Sinopic earth given
to the red earth (μίλτος) of Cappadocia used for
making pencils[1] and exported to Greece and Italy
from Sinope. It was still however noted for its
tunny fisheries and its maple and mountain nut-
trees (ὀροκάρυον), used for making tables (orbes)[2].

In the Graeco-Roman period the trade of Cappadocia went west to Ephesus, so that the ports east
of Cyzicus were not very important with the exception of Amisus. The same may be said of those on
the south coast, Attalia, Side and Seleucia : they
only served the trade of the coast-plain up to the
Taurus.

With regard to river traffic little need be said,
as the rivers, generally speaking, are swift and apt
to be dried up in summer. Yet Strabo mentions
the Pyramus[3] as navigable, also the Sangarius[4] ; the

---

[1] Strab. xii. 2, 10.   [2] Ibid. xii. 3.
[3] Ibid. xii. 24.   [4] Ibid. xii. 3, 7.

Cestrus was navigable, certainly up to Perga, also the lower courses of the Maeander, Cayster and Hermus. We may add to the list the Cydnus, the river of Tarsus on which Cleopatra "first met Mark Antony[1]." On the southern coast the rivers were often dangerous through floods; in the mountains of Pisidia an inscription has been found which records a dedication and thank-offering to Jupiter, Neptune, Minerva and all the gods, for escape from drowning in a swollen river[2]. This adds point to the "perils of rivers" mentioned by St Paul.

St. Paul in Asia Minor. Of St Paul's journeys in Asia Minor[3] we have indeed fuller details than for any other traveller in the first century. He made three distinct journeys in the west and south-west districts of the country. The first lasted for two years probably, from the spring of 47 A.D. to the late summer of 49 A.D. The months between April and July seem to have been spent by St Paul and his companion Barnabas in Cyprus, Salamis and Paphos being specially mentioned. From Paphos they sailed to the Pamphylian coast and up the river Cestrus to Perga. Their stay here does not seem to have been long; soon, probably by way of Adada, they made to the north for the Pisidian Antioch, where they taught without opposition, indeed with success, till the Jews "raised persecution against them and expelled them out of their coasts." The next place mentioned by St Luke is Iconium: as to the route

---

[1] Shakespeare, *Ant. and Cleop.* II. ii.

[2] Ramsay, *St Paul the Traveller*, &c. p. 23.

[3] See *St Paul the Traveller.*

they took thither different views are held. Prof.
Kiepert thinks that they went over the Sultan Dagh
to Philomelium on the Eastern Highway, thence
to Laodicea Combusta, then by a branch road to
Iconium. Prof. Ramsay holds that they travelled
nearly due south for some six hours by a new Roman
road to Neapolis, thence to Misthia on the eastern
shore of Lake Caralis, whence is a hill road leading
to Iconium in twenty-seven hours. This route is
both easier and shorter than that *viâ* Philomelium[1].
At Iconium as at Antioch they were first welcomed,
then expelled, and forced to escape to Lystra and
Derbe, "cities of Lycaonia and the region that lieth
round about[2]." Lystra was the easternmost of
those old cities which had been remodelled as
Roman colonies to pacify Pisidia and Isauria[3]: its
site was discovered by Dr Sterrett in 1885, the
modern name being Khatyn Serai, and the distance
from Iconium (Konia) six hours in a S.S.W. direction.
Derbe was probably at the modern Gudelissin, three
miles W.N.W. from Zosta, and was the frontier of the
Roman province on the S.E. They were both
situated in the district officially known as Lycaonia

[1] The evidence is fully stated in *St Paul the Traveller*. It
consists of

(1) An inscription found at Comana (*C. I .L.* 6974) commemo-
rating the making of a "royal road" made at Augustus' orders by
his legatus Cornelius Aquila: two such roads existed, (1) Olbasa-
Comana-Cremna, (2) Parlais-Lystra.

(2) A reference in the 'Acts of Paul and Thekla.' Onesiphorus
living at Iconium went as far as the royal road leading to Lystra
and stood waiting for St Paul.

[2] Acts xiv. 6.   [3] See above.

Galatica, *i.e.* that part of Lycaonia which was comprised in the province of Galatia. Similarly Iconium was a city of Phrygia Galatica. The preaching at Lystra and Derbe must have occupied the autumn months of 48 and the early part of 49 ; then the travellers returned by stages, through Lystra, Iconium, Antioch and across Pisidia, up to May probably, and after a short stay at Perga returned by Attalia to the Syrian Antioch.

The second journey was not confined to Asia Minor, though it began there. St Paul and Silas in the early summer of 50 A.D. probably "went through Syria and Cilicia confirming the churches," and then, doubtless through the Cilician Gates, came to Derbe and Lystra[1]. St Paul's movements on this journey have been the subject of keen controversy. St Luke goes on to say that they went "through the cities delivering the decrees ordained of the apostles and elders which were at Jerusalem," and that "they went throughout Phrygia and the region of Galatia." With this statement must be coupled the passage in the Epistle to the Galatians which states that "through infirmity of the flesh" St Paul first preached to them. The theory most usually adopted[2] is that by "Galatians" are here meant the inhabitants of Galatia in the old, narrow sense, viz. that part of the great Roman province which had been the original kingdom of Amyntas. This was a

---

[1] Acts xvi. 1.

[2] The best brief statement of this view is to be found in the Introduction to Bp Lightfoot's *Epistle to the Galatians*.

sparsely populated district, hot and dusty in summer and covered with snow in winter.

The objections to this view are many. First, the Roman province of Galatia comprised, in addition to Galatia proper, parts of Phrygia and Lycaonia: the inhabitants of the province had to be called by some name; if St Paul in writing to them had called them Phrygians or Lycaonians he might as well have said " slaves " and " robbers " at once, for Phryx was a common slave-name and the Lycaonians were in the worst repute for brigandage. Again, it is strange that St Paul should depart from his usual custom in seeking out the great cities in which to begin his work, and should visit a number of places such as Ancyra, Tavium or Pessinus, where he would not be understood by the Gallic population without an interpreter. The climate too would be most unsuitable for an invalid, as he clearly was at the time. Far more probable does it seem that by Galatians are meant the inhabitants of Phrygia Galatica and Lycaonia Galatica, men who spoke Greek, and were able to appreciate Christian teaching as the rude northerners could scarcely have done. In fact, later history shows that Paganism continued dominant in North Galatia till the third or fourth century. It is not unlikely that St Paul's infirmity was malarial fever, which is endemic in the enervating climate of Pamphylia. The cure recommended would be either a sea-voyage or removal to the interior, and he chose the latter alternative as not likely to interrupt his work so materially.

After spending the summer then in preaching in the district already visited during the first journey, St Paul and Silas were "forbidden of the Holy Ghost to preach the word in Asia"; when they had reached Mysia (doubtless by the Eastern Highway and its branches through Phrygia) they were similarly prevented from visiting Bithynia, though this could easily have been done by the road from Dorylaeum to Nicomedia. At Troas came the vision to St Paul of the "man of Macedonia," leading to his journey, still with Silas, to Macedonia and Achaia. This seems to have lasted from the autumn of 50 to the spring of 53.

The third journey began in the summer of 53, immediately after the Apostle's fourth visit to Jerusalem and his brief stay in the Syrian Antioch. After passing through the Cilician Gates he must have spent July and August in "going over all the country of Galatia (τὴν Γαλατικὴν χώραν) and Phrygia in order, strengthening all the disciples[1]." His aim on this occasion was to break new ground in Asia, that province which had been forbidden to him on his second journey. Ephesus, as the centre of the road-system, would be his natural starting-point: from Derbe and Lystra it could be reached either through Antioch to Apamea and Laodicea (i.e. along the great highway) or through Cappadocia and Northern Galatia. The former route was so much more usual that it would be implied unless any other were specially mentioned. There

[1] Acts xviii. 23.

is however one slight difficulty to be noticed. If St
Paul travelled by the great trade-route, he must
have passed through Colossae, ten miles distant from
Laodicea. Yet in the Epistle to the Colossians
he definitely states that he had not seen them nor
the Laodiceans "in the flesh[1]." It is however
possible that a traveller on foot as St Paul doubtless
was on all his journeys in Asia Minor, might prefer
the shorter route across the plain of Metropolis
through Eumenia and down the Cayster valley.

The stay at Ephesus occupied more than two
years (probably October 53 to January 56). The
number of Churches addressed in the Book of the
Revelation shows that much evangelizing had gone
on in the surrounding districts, though there is no
necessity to assume that all the Seven Churches
were founded by St Paul in person.

After the disturbances at Ephesus caused by
Demetrius and his fellow-craftsmen, St Paul "de-
parted for to go into Macedonia[2]." Thence he struck
south for Achaia, then back to Philippi, whence a five
days' voyage took him and his companion, St Luke,
to Troas. Here a stay of seven days was made,
at the end of which St Luke and seven others sailed
round the Troad to Assos, whither St Paul journeyed
on foot. He then went on board and sailed past
Mytilene, Chios and Samos, making a brief stay
at Trogyllium. After the farewell at Miletus to the
elders of the Ephesian Church, the voyage continued
by way of Coos and Rhodes to Patara. There

---

[1] Col. ii. 1.   [2] Acts xx. 1.

a Phoenician ship was found which had a good run
along the west coast of Cyprus to Tyre. This was
the last journey of St Paul in Asia Minor, or at any
rate the last of which we have any knowledge.

Spread of
Christi-
anity in
Asia
Minor.

This mere sketch of St Paul's travels brings out
at any rate some facts of cardinal importance for the
history of the Early Church. First he used all the
facilities offered for easy communication, as far as he
could ; secondly he aimed at visiting the cities which
were the centres of life and thought. In pursuance
of this aim we find that he made his longest sojourn
at Ephesus. Unconsciously he was following the
policy of the Macedonians and the Romans when
they sought to spread civilization in the backward
districts by means of colonies. The Macedonians
had done something to spread Hellenic culture, the
Romans did far more, but it was left to Christianity
to raise the inhabitants of Asia Minor out of semi-
barbarism. "Christianity," says Prof. Ramsay[1],
"conquered the land, and succeeded in doing what
Greece and Rome had never done ; it imposed its
language on the people."

The new religion spread most rapidly in districts
already Hellenized. In cities like Ephesus and
Antioch, open to new ideas and accustomed to the
moral teaching of philosophers, Christianity took
root : but where Greek education had not spread
it made no progress. Hence its development
followed the great lines of communication in the
Empire, the chief being the route from the Syrian

[1] *H. G. A. M.* p. 24.

Antioch, where "the disciples were first called Christians," through the Cilician Gates and across Lycaonia to Ephesus. Subsidiary to this was the route through Philadelphia to Troas, whence Rome could be reached by the Via Egnatia and Brundisium; also that through the Cilician Gates to Tyana, Caesarea and Amisus[1].

Asia Minor was the highway by which Christianity passed to the capital of the world; for a hundred years after St Paul's death it was the spiritual centre of the new faith. Now all is changed; the tide of Christianity, as of empire, has set westward, and Anatolia is but a broken shrine for the memories of the past.

[1] Ramsay, *Church in the Roman Empire.*

CHAPTER VI.

EFFECTS OF COMMUNICATION.

IN conclusion two questions need some answer :— What effects had this system of intercourse on government, commerce, and social life? and Why did it fail to last? To give a complete answer would be to write a history of the Roman Empire or rather of European civilization to the present day. Yet each student may work out some fragment of the truth. From the point of view of government, we may say that the Roman system of communication by sea, and still more by land, drew tight the bonds of empire. The Roman roads were the symbol of the mistress city to the provincials who might never visit her, and perchance could not even speak her tongue. The Romans had grasped one of the great secrets of government, that the mass of men are swayed by their imagination rather than by their reason; the roads from north and south, east and west, all converging at Rome, pointed more eloquently than official proclamation or sophists' harangue to the unity of the Empire.

Yet this unity was far from perfect; that East and West had little really in common is shown by the foundation of Constantinople; and even in the first century the imperial policy had to battle with the exclusive spirit of the republicans, who regarded Rome still as a city-state, with dependencies indeed as Athens before her, but with dependencies that must never rise to be anything more. Of this spirit Juvenal and Tacitus may serve as types; they cared little for the new world that was growing up around them. Court intrigue and city vice seemed to them better worth describing than the government or the social life of the provinces. Even when Tacitus describes the German tribes he has his thoughts fixed on the Romans with whom they so strongly contrasted. To Juvenal one of the worst tokens of the degradation of the times is that "the Syrian Orontes has flowed into the Tiber," in other words, that the provinces had begun to react upon Rome.

The survival of this exclusive city-spirit, this dislike to intercourse with other lands, is curiously portrayed in a passage of Philostratus' romance. The incident is probably invented, but it points to a feeling which was undoubtedly entertained by some. "A young Lacedaemonian, descended from Callicratidas, was accused of transgressing the laws of Sparta. He had sailed to Carthage and to Sicily in vessels of his own construction and was so devoted to naval affairs as to forget those of his own country. Apollonius asked him if the mode of death of his great ancestor had not given him an aversion to the

sea, ' No,' he said, ' I do not fight.' Apollonius then
descanted on the woes of merchants and mariners,
and so worked on the young man's feelings that " he
wept bitterly when he became sensible of his own
degeneracy and quitted the sea where he had spent
the most part of his life.   As soon as Apollonius
found that the youth had come to his right mind
and gave his preference to the landed interest, he
introduced him to the notice of the ephors and
obtained his acquittal and pardon."

There is no need to say that Juvenal and Tacitus
failed to read the signs of the times : Rome and
Italy could be exclusive no longer.   The roads that
strengthened their hold on the provinces strengthened likewise the hold of the provinces on them, till
at length the Caesars themselves were the once-
despised provincials.

Commerce naturally benefited by improved communication, but one may well doubt whether
increased luxury was not bought too dear.   The
spices and jewels, the silks and frankincense of the
East had to be paid for in coin, since the products
of the West were in little demand.   Hence the
constant drain of silver to the East, which in a
century or two brought the Empire to the verge of
bankruptcy.

Socially, ease of travel promoted the spread of
new ideas and of all that is meant by that vague
word civilization.   Not only Christianity, but
philosophy and Eastern mysticism travelled along
the highways of the Empire.   Other citizens besides
the Athenians spent their time " in nothing else, but

either to tell or to hear some new thing[1]." The
great cities of the Empire were, so to speak, whirl-
pools in which met opposing currents of thought.
Paul the Christian preacher, Dio the heathen mo-
ralist, Apollonius the wonder-worker with his strange
medley of Greek philosophy and Eastern magic, may
all have visited Ephesus within a few years of one
another. Perhaps in this mingling, more than in
any other respect, lies the fascination of the epoch,
which saw the birth of the new world and the beginning of the end for the old.

"The beginning of the end ":— this brings us to
the second question, "Why did the great system of
intercourse fail to last?" It was of course bound up
with the existence of the Empire and fell with its
fall in the West. The Empire in the East still kept
up the old imperial traditions: the roads in Asia
Minor were maintained as well as ever, perhaps even
better, because they were now military as well as
commercial highways. But in the West the system
slowly crumbled away. May one cause have been
that it was too complete in one sense and not
complete enough in another, that "all roads led to
Rome" and few from province to province? Where
Rome failed was in not binding her subjects together.
Gaul and Greek, Asiatic and Spaniard, were linked
with Rome, but not with one another. Again, the
very ease of travel over the known world tended to
educate the future conquerors of Rome. "The
barbarians would not have conquered, had they been

[1] Acts xvii. 21.

merely barbarians[1]." Those who served in the Roman armies or as slaves in Roman households carried back to their distant homes ideas which stood their descendants in good stead when they established the barbarian kingdoms of the sixth century.

When Rome grew powerless, her system of intercourse was bound to fall to pieces. Perhaps the most striking instance of this is seen in the strange legend told by Procopius of Britain. The island had in the fifth and sixth centuries "passed completely out of the sphere of the Empire's consciousness[2]." The story went that "the fishermen and farmers who live on the northern coast of Gaul pay no tribute to the Frank kings, because they have another service to perform. At the door of each in turn, when he has lain down to sleep, a knock is heard, and the voice of an unseen visitant summons him to a nocturnal labour. He goes down to the beach as in the constraint of a dream, and finds boats heavily laden with invisible forms, wherein he and those others who have received the supernatural summons embark and ply the oars. The voyage to the shore of Brittia is accomplished in the space of an hour in these ghostly skiffs, though the boats of mortals hardly reach it by force of both sailing and rowing in a day and a night. The unseen passengers disembark in Brittia, and the oarsmen return in the lightened boats, hearing as they depart a voice speaking to the souls[3]."

---

[1] Arnold, *Roman System of Provincial Administration (ad fin.).*
[2] Bury, vol. II. *History of the Later Roman Empire*, pp. 32,33.
[3] Bury, p. 53.

In the Middle Ages legend was busy with the remains of Roman skill. The origin of the great Limes Germanicus was wholly lost; it was counted as the work of the Evil One and called the Teufelsmauer. Asia Minor, after the era of the Crusades, was unvisited by western travellers for centuries till it was opened up to some extent by explorers sent out under Louis XIV. For Roman life in this and other lands the words of Ajax hold good :—

...ὁ μακρὸς κἀναρίθμητος χρόνος
φύει τ᾽ ἄδηλα καὶ φανέντα κρύπτεται.

Yet Time, though he hides much, reveals much too; and year by year throws more light on that marvellous system which for ages helped to make Rome the centre of the world.

INDEX.

10—2

For EU product safety concerns, contact us at Calle de José Abascal, 56–1°,
28003 Madrid, Spain or eugpsr@cambridge.org.

www.ingramcontent.com/pod-product-compliance
Ingram Content Group UK Ltd.
Pitfield, Milton Keynes, MK11 3LW, UK
UKHW020315140625
459647UK00018B/1880